Distributed By
The Nutri Books Corp.
Box 5793
Denver, Colorado 80217

HONEY
I LOVE YOU

(You're so sweet and good to me.)

HONEY
I LOVE YOU

(You're so sweet and good to me.)

Rev. Maurice H. Ness

Royal Publications Inc.
Denver, Colorado
U.S.A.

Printed in the United States of America

ISBN 0-918738-00-8

To
My Dear Wife Randi

PREFACE
TO THE REVISED EDITION

The many benefits of honey described by Reverend Ness in the First Edition of HONEY, I LOVE YOU still hold true. On the other hand, science has lengthened the lists of known problems related to the use of refined sugar and its frequent chemical substitutes. Ailments linked to either sugar or synthetic sweeteners now include very serious degenerative diseases. Using honey instead of the alternatives may not provide the whole answer, of course, but it's certainly a step in the right direction. People who care are shying away from foods that are heavily processed to seek those in a more natural state with the original goodness left in. Such people are doing themselves and their families a favor by choosing honey rather than the calorie or chemical laden and non-nutritive alternatives. The requests of these concerned individuals for new and better recipes have resulted in this revised edition of HONEY, I LOVE YOU.

The goal of this book is to give reasons for cooking wholesomely with honey and to make it easier than ever with many simplified and varied new recipes. For example, this revised edition contains new sections with delicious recipes for meats, vegetables, fresh fruit desserts, dressings, pies, sauces, rolls and miscellaneous items. You'll find tasty recipes for everything from Apricot Nut Loaf to Zesty Meat Sauce. What's more, all recipes have been kitchen-tested. Now, even the less experienced cook can use honey to prepare outstanding dishes.
Enjoy!

Roger Willbanks
Editor

Special thanks to: Barbara Farr, Bill Polvogt and the Canadian Beekeepers.

FOREWORD

This is the fascinating story of how the bee manufactures honey, and what medical and scientific observers through the ages have to say about this wonderous substance.

Honey is a marvelous nutrient that carries health in every drop, and from the use of which it is impossible to imagine anything undesirable. Can this be said about any other food? Food? Yes, indeed! For honey is much more than just a "condiment" or "sweetener" as most people regard it.

In my lifetime of close contact with people in their homes and at work, in illness and poverty, in the concentration camps during World War II, I have seen results from the use of honey as food and medicine that I could describe only by the word "miraculous".

Honey is indeed a still untapped treasure-chest of nourishing and health-giving substances. And the bee that produces it is a creature whose talents have intrigued and baffled the finest minds of the ages.

I have written this book to share with you my admiration both for the bee and for what he produces, and in praise of God who hath createth all things.

. . Rev. Maurice H. Ness

INTRODUCTION

A wise man once said that "the people" is like an art collector or a jewel collector—choosing, preserving, polishing, and carrying over the decades only that which is truly beautiful or valuable.

Indeed, in the course of centuries the people have used many natural substances in the belief they could heal. Many of these failed the test of time and have been forgotten. Honey, however, continues to enjoy a well-earned and growing reputation for medical efficacy and is being increasingly used throughout the world.

For many centuries honey has been regarded as a wonderful gift of nature in which are combined both the properties of an excellent food—a delicacy, in fact—and many healing values. Back in time as far as Hippocrates, and beyond, ancient medical manuscripts have attached great importance to honey as a medicine.

Folk medicine has used honey from time immemorial. Now the results of experiments and observations made by medical and biological scientists in recent years indicate that honey may truly possess a host of therapeutic properties and may soon take its place in the clinic alongside the many other natural and herbal healers that folklore has contributed to the modern pharmacopoeia.

In any event, honey is a substance that almost everyone from the infant to the aged can use—whether for food or for medicine—with the greatest of pleasure, with no fear of harm or "side-effects", and certainly with a minimum of cost.

Contents

HONEY AND FOLK MEDICINE

Medicine is one of the oldest of the sciences. Thousands of years ago primitive man, who was close to nature, began—purely by trial and error—to use various forces and gifts of nature as a means of curing disease.

Observation and folk wisdom have done much to advance medicine. Many drugs, including digitalis, adonis, quinine, opium, otropine, and cocaine, have been refined from herbal folk medicine. Even such a drug as penicillin was successfully used in folk medicine many decades ago in the form of green mould.

Hippocrates wrote: "You must not be ashamed to ask common people if something seems useful to them as a remedy, because I think that the art of medicine as a whole was discovered in that way".

In Europe, folk medicine is thought of highly both by people and by physicians, and has been studied by men like St. Botkin, G. Zakharyin, A. Ostroumov, V. Massein and others of prominence in the scientific community.

V. Massein always said that though many drugs have been evolved by scientists, medicine still draws much of its knowledge from folk medicine.

AN ANCIENT REMEDY

Ancient medical books offer dozens of prescriptions in which honey is given a prominent place. It is prescribed with herbs such as chamomile, nettle, colts foot, parsley, hops, onions, mustard seed, garlic, poppy seed, vinegar, and so on. Honey is spoken of as a remedy freely given to the old and young, even to the woman big with child.

Many doctors today recommend that honey be used to sweeten milk for the food of babies. Honey is palatable and digestible as well as nutritious. It also has a definite beneficial influence upon the retention of calcium by infants. Your physician can supply you with a baby's feeding formula using honey. Honey is an excellent source of readily available energy for growing children.

As a wonderful medicine, honey is lauded in epic poems, folk songs and tales. Honey was the medicine used by the first folk physician-wise ancients who had stored a wealth of experience. Epic tales tell us how these ancients cured Ilya Muronets, the legendary knight, who "sat stone-still" in the village of Karacharovo for thirty-three years. They "Gave him a cup of mead" and he found his former strength returning to him. Karevala, the Karelo-Finnish epic, also gives many vivid instances of cures performed with honey.

AMBROSIA & GLUCOSE

And everyone is familiar with the life-giving "Ambrosia", legendary "Food of the Gods" in Greek mythology. It is believed that "ambrosia" was some form or type of honey. Before examining what the healthful properties of honey are, let us consider the curative properties of ordinary glucose or grape sugar, the chief constituent of honey.

Glucose is widely used in medicine for cardiovascular diseases, hypertention, hemorrhage, (particularly gastric) stomach ulcers, children's intestinal diseases, various infectious diseases, such as scarlet fever, typhus, dysentery, malaria, sore throat, measles, and for sepsis. Glucose is the most effective medicine for poisonings. There are many other ailments which are effectively treated with glucose. In addition to being an excellent food for cells, tissues and organs, glucose increases the glycogen content of the liver, the source of the organism's energy, and improves metabolic processes in the tissues.

It acts as a tonic on the cardiovascular system when there is a decreased sugar content of the blood. In modern therapy, glucose is widely used to intensify the detoxifying activity of the liver.

Once we realize that honey, in addition to glucose, contains mineral salts, organic acids and other substances necessary for life, the source of its potential therapeutic and prophylactic value becomes clear.

14

NATURE'S HONEY FACTORY

What an interesting sight it is to see bees on a warm summer day hovering over flowers gathering drops of sweet nectar from them. It all seems so simple and serene.

But far from it! To produce a hundred grams of honey, a bee must visit *a million flowers*. With her tongue, or proboscis, a bee sucks up nectar. When her honey-stomach is full, she flies back to her hive. A bee can fly at the speed of 130 miles an hour, and that is as fast as the fastest train. Even when she carries a load equal to three quarters of her weight she can develop a speed of 60 miles an hour.

A FREIGHT PROBLEM

To manufacture two pounds of honey, a bee must bring from 120,000 to 150,000 loads of nectar. Suppose that the flowers from which the bee collects nectar are located a mile and a half away from the hive, then the bee has to fly 3 miles with each load—altogether a distance equal to 8.5 to 11 times the distance around the equator.

When the bee arrives at the hive, she gets in through the bee-entrance and must pass the "sentries" guarding the entrance against strange bees or other insects. In the hive the forager is met by "house-bees" which receive the nectar. For some time the nectar is kept in the "house-bee's" honey-stomach, where it is further processed. The processing starts in the forager's stomach on the way from the flowers to the bee-hive.

The "house-bee" opens her mandibles sidewise, stretches her proboscis forward and downwards, and a droplet of nectar appears at the tip of the proboscis. Then she again drops the drop into her honey-stomach and folds back the proboscis.

LOW-SPEED PRODUCTION

The regurgitation and swallowing of the drop of nectar is repeated from 120 to 240 times, after which the bee finds an empty hexagonal cell and deposits the drop in it. But this is still nectar, and before it becomes honey other bees will carry on the processing.

When "house-bees" are too busy, the foragers themselves attach their load, a drop of nectar, to the hexagonal cell-wall. This is very important from the practical point of view, as hanging drops have a larger surface area, which facilitates the evaporation of moisture from the nectar. Nectar contains from 40 to 80 per cent moisture, and sometimes as much as three quarters of it must be removed to produce honey.

To achieve this end, bees carry every drop of nectar several times from one cell to another, until part of the moisture is evaporated and the green honey becomes viscous. Evaporation is facilitated by the work of many bees, which, by fanning their wings, (a bee flaps its wings 26,400 times a minute) sets up additional circulation of air in the hive.

In addition to this purely mechanical concentration of nectar through evaporation, it is also concentrated in the bee's honey-stomach. Researchers such as Kabloukov hold that the cells of the honey-stomach absorb water, which goes into the system and is ejected from the body. In this way the drop of nectar diminishes in the body of the worker-bee, as its water is absorbed by the cells of the honey-stomach. Then it receives enzymes, organic acids, disinfectants and some other substances.

RIPENED & "CANNED"

From the honey-stomach the drop of nectar is again transferred to a cell, and the procedure is repeated until the nectar becomes honey. Ripe honey contains no more than 18 to 20 per cent moisture.

When cells are filled with honey, bees seal the cells with wax caps, and in this fashion honey can be kept for many years.

(Wax is a secretion from the worker bee.)

A bee colony, which consists of up to 80,000 bees, can produce as much as 300 pounds in a season.

When bees are given the opportunity of collecting nectar from flowering plants of one variety, the honey they produce is more or less homogeneous and is named after the plant from which it has been collected.

Comb honey has the best flavor and is the most expensive because it comes in natural packing, the comb, made by the bees themselves.

There is a special kind of honey which the bees produce from vegetable and animal sources, such as "honey dew" appearing on some plants and the high-sugar content liquid excretion of certain insects. Bees readily collect these excretions and the honey they make from them is used mainly in confectionary and the brewing industry. Without laboratory tests, only a taster can tell by a peculiar scent if honey contains an admixture of honey-dew honey.

HONEY, THE TREASURE CHEST

ENERGY

All living organisms, from the simplest single-celled plant or animal on up to Man, the complex, must have nourishment in order to exist. The nourishment should be suitable to the organism, and readily assimilable, once it is ingested. It goes without saying that while all living organisms prefer the *most* suitable nourishment, they do not always get just that, but often must make do: the body converts the substance given it to a more use-able form.

For Man, honey is a veritable treasure-chest of nutrition—considering the proportion of useable nutrient to the proportion of waste material—and by some chance of fate (though I prefer to think of it as God's plan) occurs naturally in a form that man's body finds *most* suitable. It would be difficult to name a dozen other substances, out of the thousands we use for food, of which this is true.

Of all nutritive elements for Man, sugar is the most quickly assimilated. But beet sugar, cane sugar, and glucose are assimilated by the human organism differently. Glucose is absorbed into the blood stream directly, without undergoing any changes—it may even be injected intravenously, which is done in cases of many diseases—while other sugar must first be broken down into its simpler components.

The hydrolysis of sugar takes place in the small intestine, where it is broken down into glucose and levulose by the digestive juices; these simple sugars are absorbed into the blood of the portal vein, which carries it into the

19

liver, and thence distributes glucose to the tissues of the body.

Since honey consists almost entirely of glucose and levulose, it is clear what an easily digestible food it is. In addition to simple sugars, bee honey contains a number of substances necessary for the cells, tissues, and organs to function normally.

ENZYMES

The researches of I. Makayev, V. Gulevich and L. Broude show that enzymes are more perfect and subtle means at the command of living organisms than the common reagents in the hands of chemists. For example, the hydrolysis of starch can be induced by heating it with water in sealed tubes at a certain temperature; the same result can be obtained at a lower temperature if hydrochloric acid is added to starch, but a still better result is obtained with the addition of ptyalin, an enzyme of saliva.

To illustrate the efficacy of minute doses of enzymes it is enough to mention peroxidase, an enzyme the scientist A. Bach obtained from horse-radish, which is active in concentrations of even one part to 200,000,000.

Bee honey has been discovered to contain the following enzymes: diastase, invertase, catalase, peroxidase and lipase. Among foods, the enzymatic content of honey is one of the highest. Diastase (or amylase) converts starch and dextrin into sugar. Invertase converts beet and cane sugar into glucose and fructose. Catalase decomposes peroxides. Some scientists attribute the excellent properties of honey to the enzymes it contains.

MINERALS

Mineral salts are vital for human health. Experiments have shown that animals die when they are systematically given food that is lacking in mineral salts even though it may be rich in proteins, carbohydrates, fats and vitamins.

The minerals honey contains are calcium, sodium, potassium, magnesium, iron, chlorine, phosphorus, sulpher and iodine salts; some honeys contain even radium. The percentage of some salts in honey is almost equal to their concentration in human blood serum.

A spectral analysis of buckwheat and polyfloral honey in E. Przhevalski's laboratory showed that honey also contains salts of manganese, silicon, boron, chromium, copper, lithium, nickel, lead, tin, titanium, zinc and osmium.

In addition, honey contains some organic acids (malic, tartaric, citric, lactic, oxalic), proteins, a derivative of chlorophyll called zanthophyll, and other substances. In the opinion of V. Filatov, the famous ophthalmologist, honey also contains biogenic stimulants (substances increasing the activity of the body).

Experiments conducted at the Botanical Garden of Lvov University have established that honey contains growth factors (bioses). Branches cut off trees and planted after treatment with water and honey, quickly took root and grew well.

VITAMINS

While vitamins are essential food constituents, they are also used for therapeutic purposes. It is now well known that with the knowledge of vitamins man has conquered such terrible deficiency diseases as scurvy, beriberi, rickets, pellagra, hemeralopia, and others. So we can safely say that vitaminology is one of the cornerstones of modern dietetics. Without a thorough knowledge of vitamins there can be no understanding of the fundamentals of modern biochemistry and physiology.

It is now known for certain that vitamins participate in all vital processes taking place in a living body.

Honey contains a number of vitamins, such as B2, B6, Biotin, K, C, and others.

Vitamin B2 (Riboflavin) takes part in the metabolism of carbohydrates, fats and proteins, the absorption of glucose from the intestines, and helps to improve vision. Some scientists hold that riboflavin is a factor of nonspecific immunity, that it increases resistance to streptococcal infection.

Lack of vitamin B2 in food can cause the development of ulcerative colitis, increase the excitability of the nervous system, cause lesions on the skin of the face and eye diseases.

Investigations show that honey contains a considerable amount of riboflavin, almost as much as chicken meat, seventeen times as much as fresh apricots, sixteen times as much as grape juice and fresh apples, five times as much as cheese or raw carrots.

Vitamin B6 (pyridoxine) participates in protein metabolism and is an antidermatitic factor in that it prevents skin diseases. Pyridoxine is indicated in cases of neuralgia and of some disturbances of the central nervous system. Lack of pyridoxine in food may cause muscular weakness, irritability, convulsions, and even paralysis, among other symptoms.

Vitamin H (Biotin) takes part in the metabolism of fats and proteins and facilitates their assimilation. Biotin prevents the development of eczema, herpes, furunculosis, and psoriasis.

Vitamin C increases the resistance of the body to infections and participates in the processes of oxidation and reduction.

Even if the vitamins listed above are contained in honey in only small quantities, they are of immense importance, because they come in combination with other substances such as carbohydrates, mineral salts and organic acids.

The vitamin content of honey depends on the admixture of pollen. It has been established that when pollen is removed from the honey by filtration, the honey loses almost all its vitamins. Heat in processing can also destroy vitamin content. For maximum value, then, the best honey is that which has been the least heated, the least strained, filtered, or blended—in fact, the least tampered with by man in his efforts to speed production and cut costs regardless of the quality of product.

ALKALINITY

It is of utmost importance to maintain a proper acid-alkaline balance in the body.

The common acid-neutralizing alkaline elements are potassium, sodium, calcium and magnesium. Sulphur, phosphorus and chlorine are acidic.

One should plan his diet to maintain an alkaline balance, then, as an accumulation of free acids causes physiological disturbances which decrease the body's resistance.

It is now known that foods are potentional sources of either acidity or alkalinity of the body, and this determines their role in metabolism. In prescribing a diet it must be considered that fish, eggs, fats, cereals and nuts are potential sources of acidity.

Honey, on the other hand, is a potentially alkaline food and this is of tremendous importance in determining its nourishing and therapeutic properties. Darker honeys generally contain more mineral salts than lighter ones and therefore give high alkaline values.

It has been proved that the depth of color of honey (consequently, its mineral salts content) is proportionate to its alkalinity.

Thus the nutritive and therapeutic value of honey is further enhanced by its potential alkalinity, and this explains in some measure its beneficial effect in relieving gastro-enteric complaints accompanied by acidity.

Just imagine—all that! in every drop of honey. Frankly, it almost dazzles the imagination. One should carry his jar of honey home from the store not in a brown paper sack, but in some container of silk or brocade studded with gems, or a box of precious wood bound in gold—a container at least commensurate in value with its contents.

KINDS OF HONEY

There are dozens of various honeys differing in several characteristics, the most important of which are floral, regional, and technological.

The floral characteristic shows the source of the nectar: flowers or honey dew. The floral characteristic also helps us to distinguish monofloral honey (produced from the nectar of a single one of the principal honey-bearing plants such as buckwheat, linden, black locust, fireweed or sunflower) and polyfloral honey produced from the combined nectars of several honey plants.

FLORAL

It goes without saying the completely monofloral honey—honey collected exclusively from the flowers of a single plant—is very rare. For practical purposes a honey is considered monofloral when the nectar of some one plant is predominant in it. For example, the nectar of orange blossoms predominates in what we call orange honey. A negligible admixture of the nectar of other honey plants does not influence its specific fragrance, color and flavor.

A polyfloral honey derives its name from the field where the honey has been collected, as for instance, "desert", "mountain", and so forth. The regional characteristic shows the region where the honey was produced.

Technologically, honeys are, according to the method of procurement and treatment, divided into comb honey and extracted honey. Comb is the honey deposited in hexogonal cells, which are then sealed with wax cappings. This honey reaches the consumer in its natural packing, perfectly ripe and pure. Bacteriological tests have shown that comb honey is sterile. Extracted honey is obtained with the help of a centrifugal honey-extracting machine.

GRADES

The quality of honey is usually judged by its appearance, fragrance and flavor. Color, fragrance and flavor also indicates the kind of honey. There are light, medium-dark, and dark honeys. Many kinds of honeys are distinguished from each other not only by their basic color but also by a multitude of shades.

Some kinds are quite colorless—light and transparent, like water. Commercially, light honeys belong to the highest grades. A. I. Root says "the best honeys are usually spoken of as water-white, and though this is not quite correct, still it is near enough for all practical purposes without coining a new word". Some authors, however, assert that since dark honeys contain more mineral salts, chiefly iron, copper and manganese, they must, therefore, be considered as being more valuable as foods than the light sort.

FRAGRANCE

The kind to which a honey belongs can also be determined by its fragrance. Some honeys have an exceedingly delicate and pleasant scent; in the words of Rudy Panko in *Evenings On a Farmstead Near Dikanka*, "When you bring a honeycomb, the scent in the room is something you can't imagine—clear as a tear or a costly crystal such as you see in earrings". Most natural honeys have a delicious flavor, a fact which has caused poets and bards since ancient times to compare with honey all that is good and pleasant.

Thus Homer said about Nestor: "His words flow like sweet honey". Solomon compared the sweetness of love with the sweetness of honeycomb. Shakespeare likened sweet music to sweet honey.

There are many, many kinds of honey most of which are not available everywhere. The greatest variety of honeys and the most natural (least treated) honey that

26

can be put into commercial containers will usually be found at specialty stores dealing in dietetic, natural, or "Health" Foods. I'll list a few:

Alfalfa (Medicago sativa) honey is collected from the purple blossoms of cultivated alfalfa. Newly extracted alfalfa honey comes in different shades; from colorless to amber. This honey has a pleasant aroma and specific flavor. It contains 36.85 per cent glucose and 40.24 per cent levulose. (Levulose or fruit sugar, is the sweetest of natural sugars.)

Buckwheat Honey (Fagopyrum Esculentum) is dark, ranging from dark yellow with a reddish tint, to dark brown. In contrast to other honeys it has a peculiar aroma and a specific flavor. Some tasters assert that buckwheat honey "tickles your throat". Buckwheat honey contains 36.75 per cent glucose and 40.29 per cent levulose, while its protein and iron content is higher than that of light honey. That is why it is recommended for anemia. In color, buckwheat honey resembles honey-dew honey.

Carrot (Daucus Carota) honey is dark yellow and pleasantly aromatic. It is made from the nectar of the fragrant white flowers of the biennial umbelliferous carrot.

Eucalyptus (Eucalyptus Globulus Labill) honey has an unpleasant flavor but is highly valued as a home remedy in the treatment of lung tuberculosis.

Linden (Tillia) honey is one of the very best kinds of honey and is highly valued for its exceptional flavor. When it is extracted, it is very fragrant, transparent, of yellowish or pale green color. Linden honey contains 36.05 per cent glucose and 39.27 per cent levulose.

Sage (Salvia Officinalis) honey is of a light-amber or dark golden color with a delicate aroma and pleasant flavor.

Sweet Clover (Melilotus Officinalis) honey has a delicious flavor and is considered one of the best honeys. It contains 36.78 per cent glucose and 39.50 per cent fructose.

Some other fine flavorful honeys which are in wide distribution in this country are Avocado (very dark). Cactus. Mesquite, Mountain. Orange (very fragrant). Safflower, Thistle, Wildflower, and "Wild". None of these are expensive. Actually, they cost only a few pennies more than the so-called "clover" honey one sees in all the markets and which is generally simply blended

27

honey, highly filtered and clarified.

Tupelo Honey because of its special properties will be dealt with in greater detail in the chapter following.

TUPELO HONEY

Tupelo Honey—from the blossoms of the tupelo tree—
is different chemically from all other honeys. But
beyond that, its exquisite flavor and fragrance, the method of harvesting, and the primitive and romantic setting
from which it comes, combine to place tupelo honey in a
class by itself.

Since honey by its very nature, source and history is a
substance wrapped up in romance, I'm sure my gentle
readers will not mind if I allow myself a slight romantic
digression by reprinting here an article on tupelo honey
that appeared in a recent issue of Health Saver Maga-
zine, that inexpensive little treasury of facts about food
and health that is worth its weight in gold each issue.

"Deep within the primitive, virtually virgin region of a
river swamp in Florida grows the amazing tupelo gum
tree. Here, undisturbed by the influences of chemical
sprays or chemical fertilizers, these amazing trees grow
according to the laws of nature.

"The blossoms of this beautiful tree—a small char-
treuse ball that resembles a little doll's cushion—are the
source of food for thousands upon thousands of bees.
They feast upon these pure blossoms, savor their rich
nectar and turn the little dewdrops into the prized tupelo
honey.

"Only in this plush river swamp do the pure tupelo
gum trees grow in full health. These trees are the prized
possession of the Apalachicola River Valley in North-
west Florida, where beekeepers have set up bee camps

along the river for the convenience of the tiny honey prospectors.

"Picture, if you will, this rare, exotic and impenetrable jungle area—untouched, unmarred, not spoiled by mankind. Let us take a cruise to the Gulf of Mexico, up the historic Apalachicola River to the Chipola. Here, we feast our eyes on the inspiring verdure of this virgin forest. The area is rich in rare, exotic blossoms, brilliant foliage and tall trees which grow undisturbed, basking in the beauties of all that nature has to offer. Glance above, and you will discover thousands of fuzzy blooms, offering their sweetness to the honey bee, the greatest worker in the world.

"This area is as wild as in the days of the Conquistadores. The soil in which the white tupelo gum tree grows is as rich and mineral-plentiful as it has been for thousands of years. The tupelo honey time takes place only from about April 20th to about May 1st, just as it has done for many centuries. At the height of tupelo honey production, there are as many as 30,000 colonies of bees, busy with the manufacture of the delicious, unsurpassed tupelo honey.

"These bees are the healthiest of all bees in entire America. Why? Because the deep swamp and jungle-like forests in which they live are free from any sprays or chemical residues. These bees never come in contact with artificial sprays and remain healthy, vigorous, sturdy . . ."

WHAT'S IN IT?

When analyzed, tupelo honey has remarkable characteristics which make it a preeminent food product. It contains a proportion of 23% dextrose, 46% levulose with 5% sucrose. This contrasts with the ordinary proportions of average honey: 34% dextrose and only 39% levulose. The increase of levulose in tupelo honey is of extreme importance since doctors have discovered that levulose is more easily tolerated by diabetics than any other natural sweet.

In addition, the higher percentage of levulose in the tupelo honey means that it does not granulate. In tests, tupelo honey was stored for 25 years and it did not granulate. Other honeys do not have this long free-flowing quality.

TOUGH BEES

The bees which manufacture tupelo honeys are most unusual. During the cold winter months, they "hibernate". The owners will move the hives to another state where the bees are prepared for the brief period of tupelo flow during the April and May season. Early in January, the bees are brought back to the swamps and allowed to feed on such early blooming plants as titi, maple, ironwood and others. This helps to carefully strenghten and nourish the bees, to prepare them for the work in the early spring. Small wonder that we call such bees, "the healthiest bees in the world". This health is transfered to the honey which they manufacture.

When middle April comes around, the white tupelo flow is at its height. The bees have stored up their strength for this event because within 4 to 6 short weeks, many hundred thousand pounds of honey are manufactured. The bees work so frantically that many will wear out their wings during this brief time. When the season comes to an end, the owners will close the hives and the apiaries and take the bees to a warm climate where they are allowed to rest. When the cold weather comes around the bees again are returned to the Apalachicola River Valley to turn the little drops of nectar of the white tupelo gum tree blossoms into the prized honey.

TOUGH COUNTRY

The White Tupelo gum trees of Florida grow in soil that is in the heart of the one and only Tupelo County of Florida. So "pure" is this area that some sections have never been penetrated by white people. This soil remains organically fertilized by nature just as it was in the days before white men came to this country.

This tupelo honey is never filtered. It reaches you just as nature made it. There are duplications and the tupelo tree does grow elsewhere in the United States—but no other area is as pure and the soil so rich as the tupelo area of Florida.

BUT GOOD FOOD

Tupelo honey is a natural food, rich in natural sugars such as the monosaccarides, levulose and dextrose which are speedily assimilated by the digestive system. Tupelo honey is a safe and wholesome food since many bacteria which cause disease in humans cannot grow in the honey.

31

Tupelo absorbs and retains moisture and thus retards the drying out of baked goods. This valuable property is important for health. Also, tupelo honey has been regarded as an important milk modifier by pediatricians for many years. Tupelo honey will actually kill bacteria by its unique action. Since it also possesses slight laxative properties, it is a welcome food for those who suffer from constipation.

HONEY, THE HEALER

Let no one misunderstand me to suggest in any part of this book that I look with scorn or disfavor upon modern medical science, or upon the thousands of sincere, learned, and dedicated doctors of all branches of healing.

But at the same time we must be aware, as most doctors will freely admit, that they do not yet know all there is to know—or accept much of what is known. And many, to be quite blunt about it, scoff openly at the nutritional and therapeutic properties that are claimed for certain foods, as well as at the potential danger and destructiveness that many persons see in some foods and in the increased use of artificial additives, fillers, preservatives, and chemical adulterants of all kinds.

Regarding honey, let us examine some of the things that have been said about it by critical observers and trained researchers through the years, and draw our own conclusions about its benefits.

TREATMENT OF WOUNDS

About 2,500 years ago Hippocrates successfully applied honey in the treatment of various diseases, including wounds.

Pliny, the famous Roman scientist and author (23-70 A.D.) wrote that the fat of fish combined with honey is excellent for infected wounds. He also advised the use of honey for abscesses in the mouth.

Avicenna considered that honey had the property of absorbtion and recommended the application to external wounds of a mixture of wheat flour and honey without water.

Edwin Smith's medical papyrus, too, contains interesting data on surgery and treatment of wounds, with honey figuring as an important curative agent.

In later times a combination of honey and cod-liver oil was used in the treatment of significant wounds; this combined dressing was applied to the wounds for ten or eleven days, after which period the wounds healed and dense scars appeared in their place.

Honey and cod-liver oil are used for infected wounds. Y. Krinisky, a noted Soviet surgeon, obtained good results in using the application of honey-cod-liver oil ointment to festering wounds. From his clinical observations, Dr. Krinisky concluded that honey accelerates healing. He considers that honey, when applied to a wound, sharply increases the glutathione content in the wound secretion; glutathione plays a very important role in the oxidation reduction process of the body; it stimulates the growth and division of cells and in this way promotes the healing of wounds.

UPPER RESPIRATORY TRACT

The therapeutic use of honey in the form of inhalation dates from very early days. This method is particularly effective in the treatment of diseases of the upper respiratory tract, according to the observations of Dr. Y Kizelstein on 20 patients suffering from atrophic processes in the upper respiratory tracts. He used an ordinary inhaler atomizing water solutions; the liquid for this was a 10 per cent water solution of honey. Each inhalation seance lasted 5 minutes.

Of 20 cases treated with honey inhalations only 2 failed to show improvement. Dr. Kizelstein had all these cases under observation for a long time. They had previously been treated by various standard methods without any noticeable effect, he reports.

TREATING COLDS

We know that honey was used as a medicine against colds in ancient times and is today an ingredient in many patent medicines. There are many families today who buy honey only for this purpose, as it is a favorite home remedy with them. Historically, honey is a universal relief for cold symptoms not only when used as such, but also in combination with other foods or drugs.

Some authors (K. Apins, S. Kneip) recommended honey with warm milk, others (H. Hertwig, Anna Martens) observed a rapid and positive therapeutic effect from honey in combination with lemon juice, one lemon per 100 grams of honey (one 5th of a pound). Still others (A. Oertel, E. Bauer) prescribe honey in warm sweet-clover tea, one tablespoon of honey per cup of sweet clover tea.

TROUBLES OF THE LUNG

Using honey as a remedy against lung trouble is neither new nor sensational. Hippocrates wrote that honey potion removed sputum and eased coughing.

The ancient Hindus, too, knew the value of honey as a medicine for the lungs. The Ayur-Veda says that honey with milk is the best remedy against cachexeia and consumption.

For centuries, folk medicine has used honey in the treatment of pulmonary tuberculosis in combination either with milk or animal fat. We know that about a hundred years ago people suffering from hemoptysis were given honey, both pure and in combination with carrot or turnip juice.

In spite of the opinion of orthodox medicine, there is abundant data testifying to the excellent results obtained with honey in cases of tuberculosis. This is not attributed to it any specific anti-tuberculosis properties, but rather to the fact that honey increases the resistance of the whole body and by this means helps it to control infection.

HEART HEALTH

Avicenna considered honey an excellent relief for heart pains and recommended that a moderate quantity of honey and pomegranate be taken every day by people with heart trouble. Honey has been helpful in relieving symptoms of cardiac insufficiency, angina pectoris and other diseases associated with the heart and the circulatory system.

The cardiovascular system, like the digestive system, is under the influence of the sympathetic division, but instead of being depressed or inhibited it is stimulated. The excitement which stops gastric digestion makes the heart beat more rapidly and raises the blood pressure by contracting the blood vessels.

The blood pressure, if high, may often be favorably influenced by taking two teaspoons of honey with every meal. Honey is a body sedative. It will calm down the dominance of the sympathetic division of the automatic nervous system which, when dominant, increases the blood pressure by narrowing the blood vessels in the body. Honey is a magnet for fluid. When there is a disturbance in the water balance of the body which holds fluid within the body, the taking of honey may restore it.

Pain in the region of the heart is often referred to as a "heart attack". We must remember that the heart is a muscle and being a muscle it requires sugar in order to work. It must be a natural sugar produced in a natural way such as honey which, you will remember, also contains minerals, vitamins, enzymes and something that produces a sedative effect in the human body.

If one should find that the pulse begins to skip so that pulse beats do not come regularly, taking at least two teaspoons of honey with each meal in order to lower the blood and the tissue phosphorus level and raise the calcium level may help. As one succeeds in bringing about this chemical change in the body the skipping of the pulse beat should disappear, if the body is otherwise in good health.

Symptoms of dizziness, likewise respond to a lowering of the blood and tissue phosphorus level and a raising of the calcium level. If the dizziness is of a mild nature the taking of honey could be all that is necessary.

Since honey consists for the most part of glucose, its beneficial action on the cardiac muscle is quite understandable. The honey should be a natural, uncooked and unblended type and preferably unstrained.

According to some authors, the daily consumption of about 70 grams of honey for one or two months by patients with some types of heart ailment brings about a marked improvement in their condition, normalizes their blood composition, increases the hemoglobin content and the cardiovascular tonus.

Honey has often been included in the diet of persons suffering from various diseases with signs of cardiovascular insufficiency; this provides optimum conditions for the nutrition of the myocardium.

INTESTINAL PROBLEMS

It is said that the dog is man's best friend. It is also said that honey is the stomach's best friend. Much has been written to prove that honey helps digestion. This is because the manganese and iron contained in pure unadulterated honey facilitate the digestive process and the assimilation of food. It has also been written that honey is a good remedy against constipation.

In cases of gastric and duodenal ulcers, honey should be taken an hour or two before a meal, or three hours after for relief. The best time is an hour or so before breakfast and dinner and three hours after supper. The best results are obtained when honey is taken in a glassful of warm boiled water.

Honey is very helpful for patients with decreased acidity of the gastric juice. If honey is taken an hour or two before a meal it inhibits the secretion of the gastric juice, and if taken immediately before a meal, it stimulates secretion.

LIVER

Honey has also been used in treating liver problems. Its therapeutic value is due to its chemical and biological composition. It has been established that besides being a food for the cells and tissues, glucose increases the glycogen stores of the liver and intensifies metabolic processes in the tissues.

The liver acts as a filter, detoxifying bacterial toxins, and glycogen intensifies this action, thereby increasing the body's resistance to infection. That is one reason why in clinical medicine, glucose, the major constituent of honey, is widely used for intravenous injections.

Honey has also been used in the treatment of the liver and the gall duct.

NERVOUS SYSTEM

In early Greece and Rome, physicians used honey as a sedative and a soporific.

Avicenna recommends small doses of honey in cases of insomnia; in his opinion large doses of honey could cause overexcitement of the nervous system.

Ancient medical books point out that equal quantities of mustard seed, pyrethrum and ginger, finely ground and mixed with fresh honey and used as a mouth wash or held in the mouth for some time will clear the brain of harmful rheums which cause headaches. Honey is even today in many places prescribed for relief of many nervous ailments.

WHOLE BALL OF WAX

"To wrap up the whole ball of wax" as the expression goes, let me quote to you from the writings of one of our contemporary medical doctors, Dr. D. C. Jarvis, M.D., author of the national bestseller "*Folk Medicine*" and of its sequel book "*Arthritis and Folk Medicine*", both available in almost every book store or health food store.

This particular article of Dr. Jarvis', titled "*Honey As The Ideal Food Supplement*" appeared originally in the *American Bee Journal*, and just happens to provide a perfect summary and conclusion to this chapter in my book.

HONEY AS IDEAL
FOOD SUPPLEMENT
By D. C. Jarvis, M. D.
Reprinted from the American Bee Journal

With so many articles on nutrition appearing in newspapers and magazines one becomes nutrition-conscious and tries to arrange the daily food intake so that it will contain all the human body needs. If you wish to be doubly sure the daily food intake is adequate for body needs then take two or more teaspoonfuls of honey each meal. The honey bee is, in effect, a wonderful little chemist and everything has been put in honey that seems desirable from a nutritional point of view.

To begin with, in considering the food value of honey, it contains vitamin B1, called thiamine, which is to be found in the husks of cereal grains and is therefore lacking in white bread. Secondly, it contains vitamin B2, called riboflavin, which is to be found in yeast, milk and meat, also fish and liver. Thirdly, it contains vitamin C known as ascorbic acid to be found in fresh fruits and in fresh greenstuffs. To complete the list, honey also contains pantothenic acid, pyridoxine and nicotinic acid, the latter being part of the B2 complex.

When there is a complete lack of B1 in the diet, that grave disease called beri-beri ensues, but where there is a shortage but not a complete lack of thiamine, then muscular weakness and heart weakness are frequently the result.

As for vitamin C, a complete lack of it results in scurvy, and inflamation of the gums, loss of teeth, hemorrhages under the skin and other serious conditions. All of which points to the fact that a well-balanced diet is necessary for continued good health.

In order to be sure the daily food intake is well balanced, much the best thing to do is to take honey, seeing that it possesses all the elements essential for physical well-being. Moreover, it retains these elements indefinitely, which is more than vegetables and fruits do, as unfortunately they lose some of their vitamin content within twenty-four hours after they have been picked.

The minerals in honey are even more important than the vitamins. They comprise potassium, sodium, calcium, magnesium, iron, copper, chlorine, manganese, sulphur and silica.

As these minute qualities of minerals essential for bodily health are used up in certain of the body processes, too complex to explain here, they need constantly to be replaced; hence the value of taking honey as the most simple means of getting them into the body.

We must not forget that honey contains enzymes, as they are termed; these enzymes being present in the digestive juices and in many of the tissues. Consequently, they aid digestion; yet honey itself requires no process of digestion before it can be utilized by the body. Nor can micro-organisms adversely affect it, for should they come into contact with it they are quickly destroyed.

In short, honey is a perfect food from a medical point of view. It contains no harmful chemicals and not more than one hundredth part of it is wastage. Truly, it is the ideal food supplement with which to fill in any gaps in nutrition that may be present. It should be taken each meal in order to ensure continued good health. Honey is not just another sweet. It really is a medicinal sweet that will help greatly in maintaining the health of your body and your nervous system balance.

COOKING WITH HONEY

Long before man knew anything about sugar and sugar refining, honey was his primary—if not his only—sweetener. But even today honey is still the most nutritious sweetener there is. Because of this, and also because honey adds its own piquant and inimitable flavor to foods, it is unmatched as an ingredient for almost every type of food—beverages, baking, bread, desserts, even meat dishes.

Using honey in cooking is an exciting experience and holds a challenge for every homemaker who is interested in adding new and stimulating flavors and textures to the daily diet (as well as boosting the nutritional values of her food). Onion-gravy sweetened with honey to go with boiled beef!—and suddenly the commonplace becomes gourmet fare!

For baked goods particularly the hygroscopic and antiseptic properties of honey increase the keeping qualities and freshness sometimes days beyond what you have been accustomed to expect.

Regardless of what you are cooking or baking, the addition of a little honey will pay you well in pleasant surprise, gustatory delight, and compliments from family and friends.

A FEW TIPS

But first, a few tips in the use of honey. For economy, of course, buy honey in larger quantities. The container for a five pound can of honey costs the manufacturer no more than the container for a one pound jar. You get the savings of four one pound containers when you buy a five pound can, and usually a little more to boot.

When you measure honey, measure the shortening first. Then, when you use the same cup to measure the honey, it will slide out easily. Liquid vegetable oil is more nutritious than solid shortenings.

In recipes for cake or cookies that call for sugar, you can use a lesser amount of honey instead. When you do this, put in one-fourth less liquid than the recipe calls for. (Three-fourths of a cup for each cup called for).

If your honey has granulated from cold or lack of use, simply place the containers in warm water—about as hot as your hand can stand—and let it stay until the honey liquifies again. Honey does granulate, but this does not impair its qualities at all.

HONEY RECIPES

ALL NATURAL HONEY RECIPES

Almost any recipe can be improved for flavor and wholesomeness by using fresh, natural ingredients. Such ingredients have generally been suggested in these recipes. For those times when the superior ingredient may not be available and you're willing to accept slightly less quality, you may substitute margarine for butter, white for whole wheat flour, ordinary salt for sea salt, regular baking powder for alum-free baking powder, and conventional honey for raw, unfiltered honey. But don't accept less than the best indefinitely. Full flavor and wholesomeness are worth the price.

If you're cooking on the metric system, the following table may be helpful in converting U.S. measures to metric measures.

Liquid Measure	Metric Volume Equivalent
1 tsp.	5 milliliters
1 tbs.	15 milliliters
1 cup	¼ liter
1 pint	.47 liters
1 qt.	.95 liters
Dry Measure	**Metric Volume Equivalent**
1 pint	.55 liters
1 qt.	1.10 liters
Weight Measure	**Metric Volume Equivalent**
1 oz.	28.3 grams
1 lb.	454 grams
2.2 lbs.	1 kilogram

Recipe Index

BREADS

Apricot Nut Loaf

Preheat oven to 350°

- ½ cup dried apricots cut up
- 1 cup water
- ½ cup mayonnaise
- ¾ cup honey
- ½ cup walnuts
- 1 teaspoon lemon rind, grated
- 2 cups all-purpose flour
- 1 teaspoon soda
- ½ teaspoon salt
- ¼ teaspoon cinnamon
- ¼ teaspoon nutmeg
- ⅛ teaspoon cloves

Simmer apricots in water about 10 minutes. Drain and reserve the liquid. Beat honey and mayonnaise. Add apricots, nuts and lemon rind. Add sifted dry ingredients and the apricot liquid. Mix until well blended. Bake for one hour.

Bran Bread

Preheat oven to 350°

- 3 cups sifted flour
- 4 teaspoons baking powder
- 1 teaspoon salt
- 1½ cups whole bran cereal
- ⅔ cup milk
- 1 cup honey
- 2 eggs
- ⅓ cup soft shortening

Sift together flour, baking powder, and salt. Combine cereal, milk, and honey. Let stand until most of the moisture is taken up. Add eggs and shortening and beat well. Add dry ingredients, stirring only until combined. Spread in greased 9¼ x 5¼ inch loaf pan. Bake in moderate oven for about 50 minutes.

Carrot Nut Bread

Preheat oven to 350°

  1 cup graham or whole wheat pastry flour
1½ cups unbleached flour
  1 teaspoon alum-free baking powder
  1 teaspoon salt
 ½ cup honey
  1 cup milk
  2 eggs
 ¼ cup melted butter
 ½ cup chopped walnuts
  1 cup grated carrots

Sift flours, baking powder and salt. Mix honey, melted butter, eggs, and milk. Add to dry ingredients. Mix until just blended. Fold in walnuts and carrots. Pour into greased 8 inch loaf pan and bake for one hour.

Date Nut Bread

Preheat oven to 350°

  1 cup boiling water
  1 cup chopped dates
  2 tablespoons liquid lecithin
  2 tablespoons shortening
  2 teaspoons alum-free baking powder
 ¾ cup honey
  1 egg
1½ cups unbleached flour
 ¾ teaspoon salt
  1 cup chopped walnuts

Add boiling water to chopped dates. Cream shortening, add egg, lecithin, and honey. Beat well. Add sifted dry ingredients. Mix well. Fold in date mixture and walnuts. Pour into greased 8 inch loaf pan and bake for one hour and 15 minutes.

Danish Apple Coffee Cake

    1 cake compressed yeast
    1 cup milk, scalded
    ½ cup butter
    ⅓ cup honey
    2 eggs
    3 to 4 cups flour
    ½ teaspoon salt
    3 cups sliced apples
    1 teaspoon lemon rind
    1 teaspoon cinnamon
    ¼ cup sugar
    ½ cup slivered almonds

Dissolve yeast in ¼ cup luke warm water. Scald milk, add butter, honey and salt. When cool, add dissolved yeast. Add eggs, and beat well. Add enough flour to make a soft dough. Turn out on floured board and knead. Put in greased bowl, cover, and let rise until double in bulk, about two hours. Punch down and allow to rise again until double in bulk. Roll out in ½ inch thickness and place in 9 x 13 greased pan. Scatter apple slices over dough. Mix together lemon rind, cinnamon, sugar and almonds. Sprinkle sugar mixture over apples. Let rise until almost double in bulk—about 1 hour. Preheat oven to 375°. Bake 30 minutes. Cut in squares. May be served hot or cold and with sweetened whipped cream.

Fig Bread

Preheat oven to 250°

 1 cup boiling water
1½ cups cut dried figs
 1 cup honey
 2 tablespoons shortening
1½ cups whole bran cereal
 1 egg
 1 teaspoon vanilla
1½ cups sifted flour
 1 teaspoon baking powder
 1 teaspoon soda
 1 teaspoon salt
 ¾ cups chopped nuts
 1 tablespoon milk

Pour boiling water over figs, honey and shortening and cool. Stir in bran, egg and vanilla, letting this stand until most of the liquid is taken up. Add dry ingredients, milk and nuts. Bake for about 50 to 60 minutes.

Gingerbread

Preheat oven to 325°

 ¼ cup butter
 ½ cup honey
 2 eggs
 ½ cup molasses
 ¼ cup hot water
1½ cups flour
 ½ teaspoon soda
 ¼ teaspoon salt
 1 teaspoon ginger

Cream butter and honey and add eggs—beat well. Mix hot water and molasses. Add alternately with dry ingredients. Bake in greased pan for about one hour.

Holiday Bread

Preheat oven to 375°

- 2½ cups unbleached flour
- 4 teaspoons alum-free baking powder
- 1½ teaspoon salt
- ¼ cup raisins
- ½ cup chopped walnuts
- 1 egg
- ⅔ cup honey
- 1 cup milk
- ¼ cup melted shortening

Sift flour, measure and add dry ingredients. Add fruit and nuts. Combine egg, honey, milk and shortening. Add the egg mixture to the flour mixture, stirring only enough to moisten flour. Pour into greased loaf pan. Bake at 375° for 1 hour.

Honey Kuchen

Preheat oven to 375°

- 1½ cups unbleached flour
- 1 teaspoon salt
- 2½ teaspoons alum-free baking powder
- ¼ cup safflower oil margarine
- ½ cup milk
- ¼ cup honey
- 1 egg

Topping:

- ¼ cup raw sugar
- ½ teaspoon cinnamon
- ½ cup chopped walnuts
- ½ teaspoon nutmeg
- 2 tablespoons melted butter

Sift dry ingredients and measure. Cream margarine, beat in honey, egg, and milk. Stir into dry ingredients until just moistened. Pour into greased 8" pan. Sprinkle topping over dough. Bake 25 minutes at 375°.

Iceland Holiday Bread

    1 package hot roll mix or yeast bread mix
¼ cup honey
    1 cup golden raisins

Follow directions of bread or hot roll mix. Use enough to make two loaves. Add honey and fruit to mix. Let rise as package directions say. Knead, divide dough in half and shape into 2 round loaves. Place in well greased 8 inch layer pans. Cover and let stand 15 minutes. Preheat oven to 350°. Cut a 1 inch deep circle in each loaf about 1 inch from edge. Punch down center of each loaf with hand to give traditional shape. Let rise in warm place until light and doubled in size, 30 to 60 minutes. Bake 30 to 50 minutes until deep golden brown. Makes 2 loaves.

Lemon Loaf

Preheat oven to 325°

    1 cup honey
½ cup shortening
    2 eggs
    2 cups sifted flour
    1 teaspoon salt
1½ teaspoons baking powder
¼ teaspoon soda
¼ cup milk
    2 tablespoons lemon juice
    1 tablespoon grated lemon rind

Cream shortening and add honey while continuing to beat. Add eggs, one at a time, continuing to beat. Sift dry ingredients together, add alternately with milk. Fold in lemon juice and rind. Bake in 9 x 5 greased loaf pan about 50 to 60 minutes.

Mocha Date Loaf

Preheat oven to 325°

- 2 cups sifted flour
- 2 teaspoons baking powder
- 1 teaspoon salt
- ½ teaspoon cinnamon
- ¼ teaspoon mace
- 1 cup chopped dates
- ½ cup semi-sweet chocolate bits
- ½ cup shortening
- 1 cup honey
- 3 eggs
- 1 tablespoon instant dry coffee
- ½ cup milk

Take ½ cup flour and sprinkle in dates and chocolate bits. Cream shortening and honey, add eggs, one at a time, beating well. Combine dry coffee and milk. Add sifted dry ingredients to creamed mixture, alternately with milk. Fold in floured dates and chocolate. Bake about 60 minutes in a 9 x 5 loaf pan. Cool thoroughly before trying to slice.

Orange Bread

Preheat oven to 350°

- 2 tablespoons shortening
- 1 egg
- 1 cup honey
- 1½ tablespoons grated orange rind
- ¾ cup orange juice
- 2¼ cups all purpose flour
- ⅛ teaspoon baking soda
- 2½ teaspoons baking powder
- ½ teaspoon salt
- ¾ cup broken nutmeats

Beat shortening and honey. Add egg and grated orange rind. Mix well. Add sifted ingredients alternately with orange juice. Stir in nutmeats. Bake about one hour.

Tupelo Honey Oatmeal Bread

    2 cups rolled oats
    2 cups boiling water
    1 yeast cake
    4 to 5 cups whole wheat flour
    2 teaspoons salt
    1 tablespoon kelp powder or granules
    ½ cup tupelo honey
    ½ cup luke warm water
    2 tablespoons safflower seed oil
    1 cup chopped pecans

Pour boiling water over oats and oil. Cover and let stand until luke warm. Dissolve yeast cake in ½ cup luke warm water, add honey and stir into oatmeal mixture. Add 1-½ cups flour, beat well, cover, set in warm place and allow to rise for one hour. Then add kelp, chopped pecans and enough of the remaining flour to make a dough. Knead until smooth. Place in greased bowl, cover and let rise in warm place until double in bulk—about two hours. Preheat oven to 400°. Divide dough in half and form into two loaves. Place in greased loaf pans, filling them half full. Cover pans and let rise to top of pans. Bake 15 minutes at 400°, reduce heat to 350° and continue baking 30 minutes.

White Bread

1. Put into a large pan or bowl or small plastic dishpan:
   13 cups all purpose flour
   1⅔ cups skim milk powder

2. Into a two-cup measuring cup, dissolve 2 teaspoons sugar in 1 cup lukewarm water. Sprinkle 2 packages yeast on this water. Allow to stand until it rises to the top of the two cup measure.

3. Into a four-cup measuring cup, put 5 tablespoons honey, 5 teaspoons salt, 5 tablespoons shortening, 2 cups boiling water. Stir until ingredients are dissolved, then add cold water to fill the 4 cup measure to make this mixture lukewarm. Do this when the yeast has risen to the top of the other cup

4. Make a well in flour mixture and add risen yeast and all of #3 above. Stir until well mixed and then knead until elastic. It may be necessary to add another cup of flour as you do not want this sticky.

5. Knead for about 10 minutes. Then rub shortening over surface and cover with a clean tea towel. Allow to rise until double in bulk in a draft-free place but not near heat (about three hours).

6. Grease 6 loaf pans. Knead dough down for several minutes and then cut into 6 pieces to suit pans. Knead each loaf-size piece for several minutes, rub with shortening on top and allow to rise until double in bulk (again about 3 hours).

7. Pre-heat oven to 425°, put pans in oven, close oven door, and then lower oven control to 375° for 30 to 35 minutes. Remove bread to cooking racks and rub a little margarine or butter over the golden brown tops.

Whole Wheat Biscuits (Quick Bread)

Preheat oven to 400°

   1 cup unbleached flour
   1 cup whole wheat flour
   4 teaspoons alum-free baking powder
   ¾ teaspoons sea salt
   ¼ cup honey
   4 tablespoons safflower oil
   ¾ cup soya milk

Sift dry ingredients, measure. Cut in safflower oil. Mix in milk and honey. Drop onto greased cookie sheets. Bake 12-15 minutes. Serve with honey butter.

Honey Butter:

Blend ¾ cup soft butter and 1 cup honey.

Whole Wheat Bread

Mix together dry:

   12 cups whole wheat flour
   1¾ cups instant dry milk
   1 tablespoon sea salt
   2 tablespoons yeast

Mix together wet:

   ½ cup safflower oil
   2 beaten eggs
   3 cups warm water (approx. 110°)
   ½ cup honey (dissolve thoroughly)

Add wet mix to dry and stir with a wooden spoon. After the dough is well mixed, stir it a bit every ten minutes or so for an hour. Then knead slightly until the dough becomes elastic. Shape the sponge into two large loaves and one small one, and place it in greased bread pans. Let rise 1 hour, then bake at 370° for 10 minutes. Lower heat to 350° and bake for 30 more minutes.

CAKES

Fruit Cake

Preheat oven 250°

    1 cup dried prunes
    1 cup dried apricots

Cover the above with boiling water and let stand 5 minutes. Drain and cut into small pieces. Pit prunes.

    1½ cups seedless raisins
    1½ cups golden seedless raisins
    1 cup blanched almonds (slivered)
    1 cup walnuts (optional)
    1 cup candied cherries (halved)
    2 cups candied pineapple (cut up)
    2½ cups mixed peel or fruit cake mix

Combine fruits and nuts and flour with ¼ cup flour.

Blend:

    1¼ cups honey
    1¼ cups butter

Add:

    6 eggs

one at a time and beat well. Mix in the fruits and stir well with:

    2½ cups sifted flour
    1 teaspoon baking powder
    1¼ teaspoons salt
    1 teaspoon soda
    1 teaspoon cinnamon
    ½ teaspoon cloves

Bake in one large or several small pans—5 hours for large cake or 2 to 3 hours for smaller.

Line cake pans with greased brown paper or wax paper. Water in a separate pan in the oven is good while the cake is baking.

Ginger Cake

Preheat oven to 350°

2½ cups sifted unbleached flour
¾ cup safflower oil margarine
2 teaspoons soda
1 teaspoon salt
1 cup sour milk or yogurt
1 teaspoon ginger
1 teaspoon cinnamon
1 egg
1⅓ cups honey

Sift flour and measure. Add dry ingredients. Cream margarine, add eggs, and beat thoroughly, blend in honey. Add flour alternately with sour milk, beating after each addition until smooth. Pour batter into two, well greased, layer pans. Bake 30 minutes. Delicious served plain or topped with whipped cream.

Nut Cake

Preheat oven to 325°

1¾ cups sifted unbleached flour
2 teaspoons alum-free baking powder
½ teaspoon salt
¾ cup butter
⅞ cup honey
3 eggs
¼ teaspoon soda
¾ cup milk
1 cup chopped walnuts
1 teaspoon vanilla

Sift flour, measure and add baking powder, salt, and soda. Cream butter and add honey gradually, beating well. Beat eggs until thick. Add to honey mixture. Add flour alternately with milk, beating well after each addition. Add vanilla and nuts. Bake in greased bread pan for one hour and 25-30 minutes. Frost with powdered sugar icing.

New Year Honey Cake

Preheat oven to 325°

½ cup seedless raisins
1 tablespoon flour
3 eggs, separated
¼ cup oil
¾ cup honey
2 teaspoons grated lemon rind
3 teaspoons instant coffee or carob
  powder dissolved in two tablespoons
  hot water
2 cups whole wheat flour (or 1¾ cups
  whole wheat and ¼ cup soy flour)
1 teaspoon baking powder
¼ teaspoon baking soda
½ teaspoon cinnamon
¼ teaspoon allspice
  pinch of cloves
¼ teaspoon salt
  sliced almonds for garnish

Oil and flour a 9 x 15 inch pan. Coat the raisins with one tablespoon flour. Beat the egg yolks until frothy. Add the oil, honey and lemon peel and the dissolved coffee or carob. Add the rest of the dry ingredients to the egg yolk batter, a little at a time. Stir in the floured raisins.

In a separate bowl, beat the egg whites until they hold their shape and then gently fold the egg whites into the batter. Pour the batter into the pan. Spread evenly and decorate the top with the almonds. Bake the cake for 1¼ hours or until a toothpick inserted into the center comes out clean. Then let it cool in the pan for about 5 minutes. Run a knife around the edges and turn the cake out on a rack. Cool completely before digging in. This cake keeps very well.

Orange Cake

Preheat oven to 350°

    1 cup honey
    ½ cup butter or margarine
    2 eggs

Beat the above together until creamy and fluffy.

Add:

    2 cups flour
    2 teaspoons baking powder
    1 teaspoon soda

alternately with:

    1 cup orange juice and water
      (juice of 1 orange)

Add:

    1 teaspoon salt
    1 cup floured raisins

Bake about 50 minutes.

Orange Filling

    1 tablespoon Flour
    2 tablespoons corn starch
    2 egg yolks, beaten
    ½ cup honey
    ¼ teaspoon salt

Mix the above in a double boiler.

Add the following, stirring constantly:

    ¼ cup orange juice
    1 tablespoon lemon juice
    2 tablespoons water

Add:

    1 tablespoon butter
      Grated rind of ½ orange or lemon

Cook over boiling water until thick.

Spice Cake

Mix with a fork in an ungreased 8" X 8" square cake pan:

1½ cups whole wheat flour
½ teaspoon sea salt
2 teaspoons alum-free baking powder
½ teaspoon cinnamon
1 teaspoon allspice
dash of ginger
dash of nutmeg
dash of cloves

Add and mix:

⅔ cup honey
1 teaspoon vanilla
6 tablespoons safflower oil
¾ cup water

Mix ingredients well, and bake at 350° for 45 minutes.

Applesauce Cake

Use spice cake recipe above, with the following variations: Add 1 cup applesauce to wet ingredients and decrease amount of water to ½ cup. Use 1 teaspoon cinnamon, 1 teaspoon nutmeg, and ½ teaspoon of cloves instead of the spices called for in the original formula. You may want to stir in a few raisins too.

Banana Cake

This is also a variation of the spice cake recipe. Add 1 cup mashed banana to wet ingredients, and decrease the amount of water to ⅔ cup. You may also want to cut back on certain spices (or even delete some altogether) according to your taste.

Spice Nut Cake

Preheat Oven to 350°

- 1¾ cup sifted unbleached flour
- ½ cup safflower oil margarine
- 2 teaspoons baking powder
- ¾ teaspoon salt
- 1½ teaspoon allspice
- ½ teaspoon soda
- 1 cup chopped walnuts
- ½ cup liquid lecithin
- ¾ cup honey
- 2 eggs
- ½ cup milk
- 1 cup raisins
- 1 teaspoon vanilla
- 1 teaspoon grated lemon rind

Sift flour and measure. Add dry ingredients. Cream margarine with lemon rind. Add honey gradually, beating well after each addition. Separate eggs and add yolks one at a time, beating well after each. Add flour alternately with milk and lecithin. Beat egg whites until they stand up in peaks. Fold them into batter. Fold in raisins and pour into greased 9 x 12 pan. Sprinkle with nut meats. Bake 30-35 minutes.

CANDY

Halloween Honey Puffs

    ¾ cup honey
    ¾ cup sugar
    2 tablespoons butter
    4 tablespoons cocoa
  11 cups puffed wheat or rice cereal
    ¾ cup coconut

Place honey, sugar, butter and cocoa in saucepan and boil to soft ball stage. Remove from heat.

Mix puffed wheat and coconut. Pour syrup over and when cooled enough to handle, form into balls. These may then be rolled in shredded coconut. Wrap in aluminum foil.

Sesame Seed Brittle

  1½ cups sugar (refined sugar for hardening)
    ½ cup honey
    2 tablespoons water
    1 teaspoon lemon juice
    1 teaspoon cinnamon
    1 cup sesame seeds.

Cook sugar, honey, water and lemon juice in a saucepan over low heat, stirring constantly, until the sugar is melted. Continue cooking with stirring until the mixture reaches 300° F on a candy thermometer, about 20 minutes. Remove from the heat and stir in cinnamon and sesame seeds. Pour the brittle onto a buttered cookie sheet in thin layer. Loosen before candy hardens. When cold, break into pieces. Makes 1½ lbs. candy.

COOKIES

Almond Cookies

Preheat oven to 300°

- ½ cup safflower oil margarine
- ¼ cup honey
- ⅛ teaspoon almond flavoring
- 1¼ cups whole wheat pastry flour

Sift flour and measure. Whip margarine, honey and flavoring. Add flour. Mix well. Drop by teaspoons on ungreased baking sheet. Leave several inches between cookies as they run. Bake at 300° for 20 minutes. Makes 1 dozen.

Alpine Spice Cookie

- ½ cup safflower oil margarine
- 1⅓ cup honey
- 2 eggs
- 3½ cups unbleached flour
- 1 teaspoon alum-free baking powder
- ½ teaspoon salt
- 1 teaspoon cinnamon
- ⅛ teaspoon allspice
- 1 cup chopped almonds
- ¾ cups chopped candied orange peel

Egg white icing. (See "Frostings" for recipe.)

Mix honey and eggs thoroughly. Sift flour, measure and add dry ingredients. Mix into honey mixture. Add almonds and candied orange peel. Chill. Preheat oven to 400°. Roll ¼ inch thick on lightly floured board. Cut into shapes. Place on greased cookie sheet and bake 10 minutes. Before cooling, brush with icing. Store one week in covered container to mellow and add flavor. Makes 4 dozen.

Carob Cookies

Preheat oven to 350°

- 1 cup margarine
- 1 cup honey
- 2 beaten eggs
- 2 cups whole wheat pastry flour
- 1 teaspoon baking powder
- ¼ teaspoon baking soda
- ½ teaspoon sea salt
- ½ teaspoon cinnamon
- ¼ teaspoon cloves
- ½ cup carob powder
- 1 cup rolled oats
- 1 cup chopped walnuts

Sift dry ingredients together. Cream margarine. Add honey gradually and beat well. Add beaten eggs. Add sifted dry ingredients, rolled oats and chopped nuts and mix well. Drop from a teaspoon onto a greased cookie sheet. Bake 12-14 minutes or just until the edges begin to brown. Watch closely as they brown quickly. Make 6 doz. cookies.

Carob Nut log

- ½ cup carob powder
- ½ cup soya powder or soya flour
- ½ cup ground mixed nuts
- ½ cup ground pecans
- ½ cup ground hulled sunflower seeds
- ½ cup hulled seasame seeds
- 1 cup honey
- 2 tablespoons oil

Combine all ingredients and mix thoroughly. Shape into a log. Roll the log in additional seeds and nuts, finely chopped, until well coated. Store in refrigerator in plastic bag. Slice to serve.

Carrot Cookies

Preheat oven to 350°

1 cup honey
¼ teaspoon soda
1 cup grated carrots
2 eggs
½ cup butter
2 cups rolled oats
1 cup chopped raisins
2 teaspoons baking powder
2 cups flour
1 teaspoon cinnamon

Pour honey and shortening or butter into sauce-pan. Heat until dissolved and boil one minute. Cool. Add sifted dry ingredients in 3 additions. The batter should be a soft dough. Chill well. Roll thin and cut with floured cutter. Place on oiled cookie sheets or cover sheet with oiled heavy brown paper. Watch these, as they burn quickly.

Crisp Honey Cookies

Preheat oven to 350°

1 cup shortening
1 cup honey
3¾ cups sifted pastry flour
2 teaspoons baking soda
½ teaspoon cinnamon
½ teaspoon cloves
½ teaspoon allspice

Put honey and shortening or butter into saucepan. Heat until dissolved and boil one minute. Cool. Add sifted dry ingredients in 3 additions. The batter should be a soft dough. Chill well. Roll thin and cut with floured cutter. Place on oiled cookie sheets or cover sheet with oiled heavy brown paper. Watch these, as they burn quickly.

Danish Peanut Butter Cookies

Preheat oven to 375°

½ cup butter
½ cup peanut butter
¾ cup honey
1 egg
1¼ cup unbleached flour
½ teaspoon alum-free baking powder
¼ teaspoon sea salt
¾ teaspoon soda

Cream butter and peanut butter. Add honey gradually, beating thoroughly. Add egg. Sift flour and add dry ingredients. Beat into butter mixture. Roll dough into 1¼" balls. Place 3" apart on greased baking sheet. Flatten crisscross style with fork dipped in flour. Bake 10 minutes at 375°. Makes 3 dozen cookies.

Date Bars

Preheat oven to 350°

1 cup honey
½ cup shortening
1 teaspoon vanilla
3 eggs
1¼ cups flour
1 teaspoon baking powder
1 teaspoon salt
1 cup dates (cut up)
1 cup chopped nuts

Mix all together and blend thoroughly. Spread in greased 9 x 12 pan and bake for 30 to 35 minutes. Cut and roll in sugar.

Fruit Tea Squares

Preheat oven to 375°

- 1½ cups unbleached flour
- 2 teaspoons alum-free baking powder
- ½ teaspoon salt
- ½ cup soya milk
- 3 tablespoons safflower oil margarine
- 1 egg
- ½ cup orange honey

Sift flour, measure and add dry ingredients. Beat egg, add honey, milk and margarine. Blend thoroughly. Add flour mixture, stirring only enough to moisten flour. Pour into 8 x 8 greased pan. Spread with cranberry topping. Sprinkle with cardamon. Bake 30 minutes at 375°.

Cranberry Topping:

- 1 cup ground cranberries
- ½ cup mincemeat
- ¼ cup orange honey

Honey Hermit Cookies

Preheat oven to 350°

- ¾ cup honey
- ½ cup butter
- 1 egg
- 2 cups flour
- 1 cup raisins
- 1 cup walnuts
- ¼ teaspoon salt
- 1 teaspoon cinnamon
- ¼ teaspoon nutmeg
- 1 teaspoon soda

Heat honey and butter until butter melts. Add spices and cool. Add egg, then dry ingredients and raisins and nuts. Drop by spoon onto cookie sheet. Bake about 10 minutes.

Honey & Bran Health Cookies

Preheat oven to 350°

1 cup dates boiled in one cup water until
soft. Remove from stove. Add 1 level
teaspoonful baking soda, stir
and cool

2 eggs
½ cup liquid honey
⅔ cup vegetable shortening
½ teaspoon health salt
1 teaspoon cinnamon
1 teaspoon vanilla
2 heaping tablespoons lecithin granules
2 heaping tablespoons whey powder
2 heaping tablespoons wheat germ granules

Beat all above ingredients with beaters. Add cooled
dates, beat again. Add:

¾ cup bran
¾ cup whole wheat flour
¾ cup unbleached white flour
1 cup coconut and mix with spoon.

Bake on greased cookie sheet until dark golden
brown. Makes about 2 dozen really large cookies.

Honey Cookies (With Variations)

Preheat oven to 350°

> 1 cup honey
> 1 cup margarine or butter
> 2 eggs
> 1 teaspoon vanilla
> 2½ cups flour
> 3 small teaspoons baking powder
> 1 teaspoon salt
> 1 teaspoon soda

Cream honey and butter until light. Add eggs, and beat again. Add vanilla, dry ingredients and beat until well blended. Drop from spoon, leaving room for batter to spread. Bake in moderate oven 12 to 15 minutes.

Variations:

1. Add 1 cup chopped nuts
2. Add 1 cup chopped raisins (floured)
3. Add ½ cup cut mixed peel
4. Add ½ cup candied cherries (cut up)
5. Add colored pineapple ring (cut up)
6. Add ½ cup coca
7. Add 1 cup coconut
8. Add 1 cup chopped dates.

Honey Wafers

Preheat oven to 300°

- 1 cup shortening
- 2 cups honey
- 2 eggs, well beaten
- ½ teaspoon salt
- ½ teaspoon soda
- 2 cups unbleached flour
- ½ teaspoon cinnamon
- ¼ teaspoon nutmeg
- ¾ cup slivered almonds

Cream shortening. Add honey gradually, beating well. Add beaten eggs and mix well. Add dry ingredients, mixing well. Fold in almonds. Drop from teaspoon onto greased cookie sheet. Bake until light brown, about 12 minutes. Makes 2 dozen.

Leif Erikson Kringle

Preheat oven to 375°

- 1 cup wildflower honey
- 1 egg
- 2 cups sour cream
- 1 teaspoon mace
- 4 cups unbleached flour
- 2 teaspoons soda
- ¼ teaspoon sea salt

Sift flour, measure and add dry ingredients. Mix honey, egg, and cream. Beat in dry ingredients. Divide dough in half, form each into a long roll. Chill rolls until ready to use. Cut off narrow slice of dough. Roll lightly with hands on lightly floured board into ¼" thick strips about 7" long. Form a figure 8 pinching ends together lightly. Place on lightly greased baking sheet. Bake 15 minutes until light golden. May also be dropped by teaspoonfulls onto baking sheet.

Lemon Drops

Preheat oven to 400°

- ¼ cup honey
- ½ cup shortening
- 1 tablespoon lemon juice
- 1½ cups flour
- 1½ teaspoons baking powder
- 1 egg

Cream honey and shortening. Add lemon juice and beat well. Add egg yolk and beat again. Add dry ingredients. Fold in the stiffly beaten egg white. Drop by teaspoon onto greased cookie sheet. Bake for 10 to 12 minutes.

Norwegian Berliner Krans

Preheat oven to 400°

- 1½ cups safflower oil margarine
- ½ cup clover honey
- 2 teaspoons grated orange rind
- 2 eggs
- 4 cups whole wheat pastry flour
- 1 egg white
- 2 tablespoons raw sugar

Sift flour and measure. Mix margarine, honey, orange rind and eggs very well. Stir in flour. Chill dough. If dough is too sticky, add more flour. Break off small pieces of dough and roll to pencil size 6 inches long. Form each piece into a circle, bringing one end over and through in a knot. Place on ungreased baking sheet. Beat egg whites until frothy, gradually beat in 2 tablespoons sugar until stiff. Brush tops with meringue. Bake 10 minutes.

Norwegian Honey Cookies

- 1 cup Alfalfa honey
- ¼ cup Barbados molasses
- 1 egg
- 1 tablespoon lemon juice
- 1 teaspoon grated lemon rind
- 2¾ cups unbleached flour
- ½ teaspoon cinnamon
- 1 teaspoon cloves
- 1 teaspoon allspice
- 1 teaspoon nutmeg

Mix honey and molasses. Bring to a boil. Cool. Stir in egg, lemon juice, and rind. Sift flour, measure and add dry ingredients. Blend into honey mixture. Chill dough overnight.

Preheat oven to 350°

Drop by teaspoonfuls on greased baking sheet. Place one inch apart. Bake 10 minutes. May be brushed with a powdered sugar glaze after baking. (Cookies may run together. Just slice them apart with a sharp knife.)

Swedish Honey Cookies

- ⅓ cup butter
- ⅞ cup honey
- 1 egg
- 1 teaspoon lemon flavoring
- 2¾ cups unbleached flour
- 1 teaspoon soda
- 1 teaspoon sea salt

Sift flour, measure and add dry ingredients. Cream butter, add egg, honey and lemon. Beat. Mix in dry ingredients. Knead into dough and chill. Preheat oven to 375°. Roll dough out ¼ inch thick. Cut into desired shapes. Place one inch apart on lightly greased cookie sheet. Bake 10 minutes. Ice and decorate as desired.

Prune Snacks

1 cup prunes, pitted
½ cup boiling water
6 oz. carob chips
2 tablespoons butter
1 teaspoon vanilla
1 cup chopped pecans
1 cup safflower oil margarine
1 cup honey   .
1 egg
2 cups unbleached flour   .
1 teaspoon salt
2 teaspoons alum-free baking powder

Cut prunes in pieces. Pour boiling water over them.
Add carob chips. Cook while stirring over low heat
until mixture is thick. Add butter, vanilla and pecans. Cool. Cream margarine, add honey, egg, and
beat. Sift flour, measure and add dry ingredients.
Mix into creamed mixture. Add cooled fruit and
nuts. Chill dough 30 minutes. Preheat oven to 325°.
Drop by teaspoonfuls onto greased baking sheet.
Bake for 15 minutes. Makes 4 dozen cookies.

Tupelo Honey Drops

Preheat oven to 375°

¼ cup sunflower seed oil
½ cup tupelo honey
1 egg
1 cup rolled oats
1 cup whole wheat flour
¼ teaspoon dulse powder
½ teaspoon cinnamon
½ cup raisins

Blend oil and honey together. Add egg and beat
until blended. Stir in rolled oats and milk. Sift
flour, measure and add dry ingredients. Add to
honey mixture, beat, add raisins and mix well.
Drop by teaspoonfuls on greased baking sheets.
Bake 10-15 minutes. Makes 2½ dozen cookies.

Western Peanut Butter Cookies

⅓ cup safflower oil margarine
⅞ cup honey
⅔ cup peanut butter
1 egg
¼ teaspoon soda
1 teaspoon alum-free baking powder
2 cups unbleached flour
½ teaspoon sea salt
½ cup chopped peanuts

Sift flour, measure and add dry ingredients. Cream margarine, add egg, honey, and peanut butter. Beat thoroughly. Blend dry ingredients into mixture. Mix in peanuts. Shape into roll. Wrap in wax paper. Chill several hours.

Preheat oven to 400°. Cut dough into ⅛" slices. Place one inch apart on greased cookie sheet. Bake 10 minutes. Makes 6 dozen cookies.

Yakima Coconut Cookies

Preheat oven to 375°

½ cup safflower oil margarine
⅞ cup honey
1 egg
1 lb. can peaches, chopped and drained
1 teaspoon alum-free baking powder
1½ cups unbleached flour
½ teaspoon sea salt
1 teaspoon nutmeg
1 cup coconut
1 cup raisins
½ cup chopped walnuts

Sift flour, measure and add dry ingredients. Cream margarine, add honey, egg, and peaches. Mix thoroughly. Mix peach and flour mixture together. Blend in coconut, raisins, and nuts. Drop dough by teaspoonfuls onto greased baking sheet. Bake 12-15 minutes. Makes about 5 dozen cookies.

DESSERTS

Baked Apples

    Baking apples
    Liquid honey
    Cinnamon
    Butter
    Commercial sour cream

Core apples and peel ⅓ way down from top. Put in baking dish and drizzle honey over apple. Add ½ inch of water to pan. Cover and bake about ½ hour.

Sprinkle top with cinnamon, more honey and a dot of butter. Put under broiler, about 4 inches from heat and broil until bubbly.

Serve warm, filling centers with sour cream.

Baked Custard

Preheat oven to 350°

    4 eggs, slightly beaten
    ½ cup honey
    2½ cups milk
    ½ teaspoon salt
    ½ teaspoon vanilla

Mix ingredients and oven poach at 350° until knife comes out clean from center of custard. Use one dish or custard cups.

Bavarian Cream

Soften:

  1 tablespoon gelatine (1 envelope)

in:

  ¼ cup cold water

Add:

  1¼ cups hot milk
  ⅓ cup honey
  ¼ teaspoon salt

Stir until gelatin and honey are dissolved. Cool and add:

  1 teaspoon vanilla

Chill until partially set. Beat until frothy.

Fold in:

  ½ pint whipping cream, beaten stiff

After the whipped cream has been added, fold in:

  1 cup drained crushed pineapple

Spoon into serving dishes and chill until firm. Yield: 8 servings

Blueberry Buckle

¼ cup butter or margarine
½ cup honey
1 egg
1 cup flour
1½ teaspoons baking powder
¼ teaspoon salt
¼ cup milk
2 or 3 cups blueberries (frozen or fresh)

Cream butter and honey, add egg. Sift flour, salt and baking powder together. Add alternately with milk to butter mixture. Place in 8-inch square greased pan. Spread blueberries on top. Mix the following ingredients to a crumbly consistency, and sprinkle on top of berries:

½ cup sugar
½ teaspoon cinnamon
⅓ cup flour
¼ cup butter or margarine

Bake at 325° for 30-35 minutes. Serve plain or with cream. This reheats nicely, too, for a tasty leftover. Just cover with tin foil and pop into the oven until warm.

Serve with honey whipped cream.

Honey Whipped Cream

Whip your cream. Add liquid honey which is at room temperature (to taste). Add 1 teaspoon vanilla. (Add honey slowly as you beat.)

Carrot Pudding

    1 cup grated carrots
    1 cup raisins
    1 cup Tupelo honey
    1 egg, lightly beaten
    1 cup grated potatoes
    1 teaspoon cinnamon
    1 cup whole wheat flour
    ⅔ cup soya oil
    1 tablespoon kelp powder or granules

Mix all ingredients together well. If you do not have a steamer, you may use pudding molds or cans with tightly fitted lids. Grease inside of cans and fill ⅔ full. Place cans on trivet in a heavy kettle over 1 inch boiling water. Cover kettle, use high heat; then as steam begins to escape, lower the heat. Steam 1½ hours. Serve warm.

Daffodil Delight

Prepare:

>   1 10-inch angel-food cake

Sauce:

>   2 envelopes unflavored gelatine
>   ½ cup sugar
>   ⅛ teaspoon salt
>   4 beaten eggs
>   1 cup water
>   ½ cup honey
>   1 12 oz. can frozen lemonade concentrate
>   2 cups whipping cream, whipped

Method:

Combine gelatine, sugar and salt in a large sauce-pan. Combine beaten eggs and water and add to gelatine mixture. Add honey. Cook over low heat, stirring constantly until gelatine dissolves and mixture thickens slightly. Remove from heat. Add unthawed lemonade concentrate. Stir until melted. Chill until partially set. Fold into whipped cream.

Rub brown crumbs off cake. Tear into bite-size pieces.

Cover bottom of 10-inch tube pan with thin layer of gelatine mixture. Then place layer of cake pieces. Pour ⅓ of remaining gelatine mixture over cake pieces. Repeat layers. Chill until firm. Unmold on serving plate. Serves 12-16.

Honey Applesauce

Peel and cut up into small chunks:

> 4 or 5 apples

Add:

> 1 cup honey
> ½ cup water
> 1 teaspoon lemon juice
> cinnamon to taste (about ½ teaspoon)

Heat slowly until apples are soft and turn mushy. Excellent served over hot gingerbread, or just alone with a bit of whipped topping. Excellent for baby-food, too.

Honey Apples

> ½ cup honey
> ½ cup sugar (white)
> ¼ cup water
> ⅛ teaspoon cream of tartar
> Apples and skewers for handles

Stir honey and sugar into water and heat to dissolve. Add cream of tarter. Continue heating, but watch that it does not boil over. Boil to 290° F. on candy thermometer or until syrup forms a brittle, zig-zag thread when dropped into cold water. Remove from heat, strain and dip apples in one at a time, twirling to coat whole apple with syrup. Place on buttered plate or waxed paper to cool and harden.

Peanut Honey Roll

> 1 cup honey
> 1 cup peanut butter
> 1½ cups skim milk powder
> 1 cup chopped peanuts

Cream honey and peanut butter together. Add milk powder gradually until a stiff mixture is obtained. Roll in chopped peanuts. Chill well. Slice as needed. This mixture is very good for stuffing dates

Jelly Roll

Preheat oven to 375°

4 eggs
½ cup honey
½ cup sugar
½ teaspoon lemon or vanilla flavoring
1 teaspoon lemon peel (optional)
1 cup plus 2 tablespoons flour
1 teaspoon baking powder
Pinch salt.

Beat eggs until light, add honey in a fine stream while beating, add sugar, beat well. Fold in sifted flour, baking powder and salt. Add flavoring and peel. Bake in jellyroll pan for 12-15 minutes. Be sure to line pan with wax paper, and grease the pan generously. Turn out on moist cloth sprinkled with powdered sugar. Spread at once with honey-orange filling, and roll while still warm. Cool in towel about ½ hour. Excellent served alone, with lemon sauce or plain ice cream.

Here is another suggestion: this dessert is more elegant, yet easy to serve at company time. Slice the jelly roll into 12 slices and arrange them in the bottom of a well buttered baking dish. Make up a strawberry jello with 1 cup water, 1 cup fruit juice (from drained can of fruit cocktail). Add 1 teaspoon lemon juice and chill until it starts to jell. Whip well; add ½ pint whipping cream (whipped stiff), 4 sliced bananas, 1 cup miniature marshmallows, 1 can fruit cocktail (well drained). Pour over jelly roll and chill overnight.
(Cream can be whipped using honey instead of sugar as the sweetener.)

Pineapple Honey Rice

> 1 cup long-grain rice (uncooked)
> 1 15-oz. can crushed pineapple (drained)
> ½ cup honey (or more to taste)
> ½ pint whipping cream

Cook rice according to package directions. Using a fork, stir pineapple and honey into hot rice. Cool to room temperature.

Whip the cream and gently fold into rice mixture. Chill.

For added flavor, add lemon juice to water that rice is cooked in.

Tupelo Honey Cheese Cake

Preheat oven to 350°

Crust:

> ½ cup safflower oil margarine
> 2 cups whole wheat flour
> 4 tablespoons water
> 1 teaspoon sea salt

Mix ingredients together as for pie crust and pat into bottom of lightly greased 10 x 12 inch pan.

Filling:

> 1 lb. cottage cheese
> 1 lb. Philadelphia cream cheese
> 1 cup Tupelo honey
> 1 teaspoon cinnamon
> 8 eggs
> 1 teaspoon vanilla

Mix cheeses and honey. Beat eggs thoroughly. Gradually beat in cheeses and honey. Blend in cinnamon and vanilla. Pour into crust and bake one hour.

FRESH FRUIT DESSERTS

Baked Bananas

>   6 bananas
>   ½ cup honey
>   1 tablespoon lemon juice
>   1 tablespoon butter
>   ¼ teaspoon salt

Place bananas in buttered baking dish. Cover with the other ingredients and bake in moderate oven for about 15 minutes.

These are delicious when served with pork or fish.

Baked Grapefruit

>   2 grapefruits
>   1 cup honey

Cut grapefruit in half. Remove seeds and center. Trickle honey over top of each. Bake in moderately slow oven 300° about 15 minutes. Serve immediately.

Freezing Fruits With Honey

Drizzle honey in the proportion of one part honey to four or five parts fruit—sliced or crushed. Whole fruits may be covered with diluted honey in the proportion of one cup of water to two cups of honey. Use enough to just cover the fruit in container.

Fresh Fruit Cup

2½ cups orange sections
1 cup banana slices
1 cup unpeeled redskinned apple slices
1 cup orange juice
dash of lemon juice
honey to taste
cherries for garnish

Simply combine and serve chilled as appetizer or dessert. 6 servings

Ginger Pears

4 fresh pears
¼ cup butter
¼ cup honey
1 tablespoon crystallized ginger
3 tablespoons water
2 tablespoons lemon juice

Quarter, core, slice fresh pears. Melt butter in skillet. Add honey, ginger, water, lemon juice. Heat to boiling. Add pear slices. Toss to coat with syrup. Cover. Cook 5 minutes or until pears are tender.

Hawaiian Cocktail

  1 package frozen pineapple
  2 large grapefruits
  1 medium-sized avocado

Partially thaw the frozen pineapple. It should still be slightly frosty. Drain and save the syrup. Pare the grapefruit with a sharp knife cutting off all the outer membrane. Then slip out the sections from between the membrane walls. Peel and dice the avocado. Combine the fruits, heap lightly in sherbet glasses and cover with this dressing:

  ¼ cup syrup from the pineapple
  ¼ cup lemon juice
  ¼ cup honey

Garnish with sprigs of mint, watercress or cubes of bright jelly. Raw cranberries can also be used. 6 to 8 servings.

Honeyed Apple Rings

  2 large apples
  1 cup honey
  ¼ cup water
  1 tablespoon lemon juice
  2 sticks cinnamon
  4 whole cloves.

Wash and core the apples. Cut crosswise into four pieces. Place in a baking dish. Mix the other ingredients and pour over the apple rings. Bake uncovered in a moderate oven until apples are done.

Melon Cocktail

Cantalope
Watermelon
Honeydew Melon
Honey
Lemon Juice

Cut balls from melons with ball-cutter or use a half-teaspoon-size measuring spoon. Arrange in sherbet glasses. Pour equal parts of honey and lemon juice over fruit. Garnish with berries in season.

DRESSINGS

Cream Honey Dressing

    2 tablespoons honey
    1 teaspoon lemon juice, or more if desired
    ⅔ cup commercial sour cream

Blend the above together & chill.

Fruit or Vegetable Dressing

    ½ cup honey
    1 cup salad oil
    ¼ cup vinegar
    1 teaspoon grated onion
    1 teaspoon dry mustard
    1 teaspoon salt
    ½ teaspoon paprika
    1 tablespoon celery seed

Beat all together until smooth adding onion and celery seed last.

Fruit Salad Dressing

    ½ cup honey
    ½ cup lemon juice
    ½ cup salad oil
    1 teaspoon salt

Shake the ingredients together until well blended.

Green Salad Dressing

1 cup honey
2 teaspoons mustard
1 teaspoon salt
2 eggs
1 cup white vinegar
1 cup water

Boil the above together and thicken with 2 table-spoons of corn-starch mixed with a little water. store in a covered jar.

Honey Dressing for Cabbage

3 tablespoons honey
3 tablespoons cottage cheese
1 teaspoon apple cider vinegar
¼ teaspoon mustard
Salt to taste

Mix the above well and serve on shredded cabbage. (Serves one)

Honey French Dressing

1 cup salad oil
½ cup honey
⅓ cup chili sauce
½ cup cider vinegar
½ cup finely chopped onion
1 tablespoon Worcestershire sauce
½ teaspoon salt

Combine all in a jar and shake vigorously.

Honey Sour Cream Dressing

- ½ cup thick sour cream
- 3 tablespoons honey
- 1 tablespoon vinegar
- 1 teaspoon salt

Combine ingredients and beat until thick and fluffy.

Spicy Salad Dressing

- 1 cup tomato soup
- ½ cup vinegar
- 1 teaspoon salt
- 1 teaspoon dry mustard
- 1 teaspoon Worcestershire sauce
- 1 small onion grated
  dash Tobasco sauce
- 1 clove garlic grated (optional)
- 1 cup salad oil
- ½ cup honey
- 1 teaspoon paprika

Shake well in tightly covered jar. Makes approximately 3½ cups.

FROSTINGS

Egg White Icing

Blend 1 cup powdered sugar, 2 egg whites, and 1 teaspoon lemon juice. Beat with electric beater for about 5 minutes.

Honey Icing

>   1 cup honey
>   2 egg whites
>   ¼ teaspoon almond extract

Boil honey until thickened (about 10 minutes). Meanwhile, beat egg whites until stiff, pour honey slowly over the egg whites, beating until thick. Add ¼ teaspoon almond extract.

Honey Orange Butter

>   ½ cup honey
>   ½ cup butter
>   1 teaspoon grated orange peel

Beat together. Chill and serve on pudding, gingerbread or graham crackers.

Honeymoon Frosting

Beat 1 egg white with dash of salt until stiff enough to hold up in peaks, but not dry. Pour ½ cup honey in fine stream over egg white, beating constantly about 4 minutes, or until frosting holds its shape. This is a delicate frosting and does not store well over night. Cake should be frosted the day it is to be served.

Mocha Cream

> 2 tablespoons butter
> 1 cup honey
> 1 cup carob powder
> 2 tablespoons cold strong coffee

Let butter stand at room temperature until soft. Add i cup honey. Blend together. Mix in carob powder. Drip coffee in, stirring constantly. Excellent for cake filling.

Picnic Frosting

> 1 cup chocolate chips
> 1 cup peanut butter
> 1 cup honey
> 2 tablespoons water

Melt chocolate. Combine peanut butter, honey and water. Add chocolate. Stir until smooth.

MEATS

Baked Sliced Ham

    1 canned ham
    ¼ cup honey
      whole cloves
    ¼ cup ketchup
    2 tablespoons prepared mustard
    2 teaspoons grated onion
    2 teaspoons Worcestershire sauce
    ¼ teaspoon grated lemon rind
    ⅛ teaspoon ginger

Slice ham about ¼ inch thick, then tie together and refrigerate until ready to bake.

Press cloves into top ham slices. Place on a rack in a shallow baking dish.

Mix together the honey, ketchup, mustard and ginger. Spread over top and sides of ham. Bake at 350° for about 1 hour. Baste with glaze several times. Serve hot or cold.

Barbecued Spareribs

    4 to 5 pounds lean, meaty spareribs
    ¼ cup soya sauce
    ½ cup honey
    ½ teaspoon ginger
    ¾ teaspoon dry mustard
    ¼ teaspoon mace
    ¼ teaspoon ground cloves
    ½ teaspoon salt
    ¼ cup sherry

Marinate the ribs overnight in covered pan.

Ribs may be done in oven with the marinade being basted over them frequently or they may be put on a spit rod and barbequed. When using a pit—place pan under the ribs to catch marinade and brush the meat frequently with sauce.

Chicken Oriental—Corn Crisped

1   2½ to 3 pound broiler-fryer chicken cut up
4   cups crushed corn flakes
1½ teaspoons salt
⅛ teaspoon pepper
½ cup evaporated milk

Sauce:

¼ cup melted butter
¼ cup honey
¼ cup lemon juice
1   tablespoon soya sauce

Wash and dry thoroughly the chicken pieces. Add salt and pepper to corn flakes. Dip chicken into evaporated milk and then roll in the crumbs. Place chicken, skin side up, in baking dish and bake 350° about 30 minutes.

Blend the sauce ingredients and pour over chicken. Bake an additional 30 minutes or until chicken is tender. Baste several times with the drippings and sauce.

Chinese Chicken

1   frying chicken, about 3 pounds
1   egg
¼ cup lemon juice
2   tablespoons oil or melted shortening
2   tablespoons soy sauce
1   tablespoon paprika
1   teaspoon salt
    pepper

Arrange chicken pieces in single layer in baking pan. Beat egg slightly. Add balance of ingredients and mix well. Pour over chicken and coat each piece. Bake uncovered at 325° for about 1 hour. Baste with the sauce. Serve either hot or cold.

Cooked Ham Square or Loaf

2½ cups ground cooked ham
½ pound ground veal
¼ cup ground lean pork
2 cups crushed corn flakes
¼ cup liquid honey
½ cup orange juice
½ teaspoon salt
½ teaspoon paprika
1 teaspoon prepared mustard
2 eggs
¼ cup liquid honey
¼ cup prepared mustard.

Combine the first ten ingredients and spread into a 12 x 8 glass baking dish. Bake about 45 minutes.

Combine the honey and mustard and spread over top of meat. Bake another 15 minutes.

Honey Bar-B-Que Spareribs

3½ to 4 pounds ribs
½ cup vinegar

Place ribs in large saucepan, add venegar and enough water to cover meat. Simmer covered 1 hour. Drain well.

Sauce:

2 tablespoons cornstarch
½ cup water
1 cup vinegar
½ cup honey
½ cup catsup
½ cup soy sauce
½ teaspoon salt

Blend cornstarch and water in saucepan. Stir in remaining ingredients and continue stirring as sauce thickens. Boil 3 minutes. Place drained ribs in single layer on grill or bake in pan in 350° oven for 30 minutes. Cover ribs with sauce; baste until brown.

Honey Pork Chops

    4 double loin pork chops
    ½ cup honey
    1 can sliced pineapple
    ¼ cup pineapple slices
    ¼ cup pineapple syrup from fruit
    1 tablespoon prepared mustard

Cut a piece out of each chop and insert ½ a slice of pineapple. Combine honey, syrup and mustard and spoon over each chop.

Bake at 350° for about 1½ hours, basting the honey sauce over meat. Remove from oven and top each chop with a pineapple slice. Return to oven to warm the fruit.

Serve with the warm honey sauce covering each chop.

Left-Over Turkey

    4 cups cooked turkey—diced or cubed

Cover the turkey with the following:

    ½ cup honey
    ¼ cup prepared mustard
    1 teaspoon curry powder
    1 tablespoon turkey dripping or butter

Bake at 350° until very hot. May be served with rice.

Pork Chops Supreme

    6 pork chops about ½ inch thick
    1 cup ketchup—heated
    6 tablespoons honey
    1 large lemon, sliced

Blend ketchup and honey. Pour over pork chops. Top each chop with a slice of lemon. Bake in uncovered pan at 325° for about 1 hour or until done.

This same sauce may be used with chicken pieces.

Zesty Meat Loaf (Muffin Style)

>   1 egg
>   ½ cup milk
>   1½ teaspoons salt
>   ¼ teaspoon paprika
>   ¼ teaspoon pepper
>   ¾ cup white bread crumbs
>   1 pound ground chuck or round steak

Beat egg slightly, add milk, seasoning, bread crumbs. Blend lightly together with ground meat.

Put 1 teaspoon of Zesty Sauce in bottom of six 3-inch muffin cups. Divide meat loaf into each cup. Shape lightly to fit cup. Bake at 350° for 20 to 25 minutes. Serve hot with rest of Zesty Sauce.

Zesty Sauce

Combine the following ingredients. Heat to use as meat loaf sauce or chill to serve as dip. Makes 2 cups.

>   1 15-oz. or 2 8-oz. cans tomato sauce
>   with tomato bits
>   2 tablespoons honey
>   2 tablespoons vinegar
>   dash of minced garlic
>   2 green onions, tops included (finely sliced)

PIES

Apple Honey Crumble Pie

Preheat oven to 400°

    1 9-inch unbaked shell
    6 medium apples thinly sliced

Arrange apples in unbaked shell, cover with following mixture:

    ½ cup honey
    ⅛ teaspoon salt
    ½ teaspoon cinnamon
    1 teaspoon lemon juice

Combine:

    ¼ cup sugar
    ¼ cup flour
    1 tablespoon shortening
    1 tablespoon butter

Sprinkle over apples. Bake at 400° for 20 minutes. Reduce to 350° and bake until apples are tender.

Suggestion: An excellent pastry for above recipe is this Cheese Pastry:

    2 cups flour
    1 teaspoon salt
    ¾ cup shortening
    5 or 6 tablespoons cold water
    ½ cup grated chesee

Honey Meringue

  1 cup honey
  2 egg whites
  ½ teaspoon vanilla
  1 teaspoon baking powder
  ⅛ teaspoon salt (or less)

Boil honey to 250° about 10 minutes. Pour slowly over beaten egg whites, beating constantly. Add vanilla and beat until cool.

This mixture may be used on pies, baked apples or puddings.

Honey Sour Cream Pie

  3 eggs, separated
  ⅓ cup honey
  2 tablespoons flour
  ½ teaspoon cinnamon
  1 cup sour cream

Beat egg yolks, add honey and beat again. Add flour and cinnamon. Mix well. Add sour cream. Raisins may be added. Cook in double boiler until thick. Pour into baked pie shell. May be topped with Honey Meringue or Honey Whipped Cream

Honey Mincemeat Pie

Preheat oven to 425°

Crust:

 ¾ cup flour
 ½ tespoon salt
 ½ cup rolled oats (uncooked)
 ⅓ cup shortening
 3 to 4 tablespoons water (cold)

Filling:

 2 cups prepared mincemeat
 ¼ cup honey
 2 tablespoons flour
 ¾ cup whipping cream
 ½ cup pecan nuts

Fit pie crust into pie pan, fluting the edges.

Fill with mincemeat. Mix the honey and flour, then add the whipping cream. Pour this over the mincemeat—sprinkle pecans on top

Bake about 15 minutes at 425° then reduce heat to 325° for another 15 to 20 minutes

Pineapple Patch Pie

Preheat oven to 425°

Pastry for 2 crust 9 inch pie
1 No. 2 can crushed pineapple, not drained
⅔ cup honey
¼ cup cornstarch
½ teaspoon salt
2 tablespoons soya butter
2 tablespoons lemon juice

Line a 9 inch pan with pastry. In a saucepan, blend together undrained pineapple, and honey. Mix in cornstarch and salt. Heat, stirring constantly until mixture boils gently. Continue cooking about 2 minutes until clear and thickened. Remove from heat, stir in butter and lemon juice. Pour into pastry shell. Cut round disks from balance of pastry. Place them on top of pie filling to resemble patches. Bake for 30 minutes or until pastry is brown.

Walnut Crumb Crust

Delicious base for cream pies or pumpkin pie.

1 cup fine graham cracker crumbs
½ cup chopped walnuts
¼ teaspoon salt
¼ cup soft butter
1 tablespoon honey

Mix all the ingredients and press into 9 inch pie pan. Bake in moderate oven about 6 minutes. Cool before adding the pie filling.

Gingersnap wafers may be used instead of graham crackers.

ROLLS

Cinnamon Rolls

Preheat oven to 400°

¼ cup butter or margarine
½ cup honey
¼ teaspoon cinnamon
2 cups bread flour
4 teaspoons baking powder
½ teaspoon salt
4 tablespoons shortening
⅔ cup milk

Melt the butter and add ⅓ cup of the honey. Pour into greased muffin tins and sprinkle a little of the cinnamon in each pan. Sift flour, baking powder and salt. Cut in shortening. Add the milk and mix well. Knead for ½ minute. Roll out about ½ inch thick. Spread lightly with cinnamon. Roll and cut in 1 inch pieces and place in muffin tins, cut side up. Bake for 20 minutes.

Sweet Rolls

Preheat oven to 400°

1 cup milk
1 teaspoon salt
2 eggs
¼ cup honey
2 cakes compressed or dry powdered yeast
about 5 cups flour
¼ cup shortening

Scald milk, add honey, shortening and salt. Soften yeast in lukewarm water and add to milk mixture. Add beaten eggs and half of the flour. Beat well. Make a well in this and add the rest of the flour. Knead on a slightly floured board until smooth. Place in a greased bowl. Cover and let rise to double the bulk. Punch down and form into rolls or coffee rings. Let rise again. Bake for 20 to 25 minutes.

Orange Rolls

    2 pkg. dried yeast
    ¼ cup luke warm water
    ¼ cup shortening
    1 cup milk
    ¼ cup liquid lecithin
    ½ cup honey
    1½ teaspoons salt
    2 eggs, beaten
    4 to 5 cups unbleached flour

Filling:

    ¼ cup honey
    2 tablespoons grated orange rind

Soften yeast in luke warm water. Scald milk. Add shortening, honey and salt. Cool, add softened yeast, eggs and two cups flour. Mix thoroughly, add enough flour to make a soft dough. Knead until smooth, place in a greased bowl, cover, and let rise until double in bulk. (About two hours.) Punch down and let rest ten minutes. Roll into a rectangle ½ inch thick. Spread honey filling over dough. Roll up jelly-roll fashion, sealing edges. Cut into one inch slices. Place slices cut-side down into well greased muffin pans. Cover and let rise until double—about one hour. Pre set oven to 375°. Bake 20-25 minutes. Makes 3½ dozen.

SAUCES

Chicken Honey Sauce

A honey sauce is scrumptious with baked chicken. One that's excellent is simply a mixture of ¼ cup melted butter, ¼ cup honey and ¼ cup lemon juice. Use it for basting during the last half hour of baking.

Fluffy Horseradish Sauce

Serve this with grilled steaks, hamburgers or roast beef.

  ½ cup commercial sour cream
  2 tablespoons prepared horseradish, drained
  1 tablespoon lemon juice
  1 tablespoon honey
  2 teaspoons chopped chives (or mild onion)

Combine ingredients. Blend well and refrigerate in covered container for 3 to 4 hours to blend the flavors.

Honey Glazed Ham—Score rindless ham in diamond design. Stud with cloves and baste with sauce during the last few minutes of baking.

Honey Sauce

  ½ cup honey
  ¾ cup boiling water
  1 tablespoon butter
  1 tablespoon cornstarch
  ¼ cup cold water

Mix cornstarch with cold water. Pour boiling water into this and cook in double boiler until clear. Add honey and butter. This may be served hot or cold.

Honey Hot Sauce

½ cup mayonnaise
¼ cup sour cream
2 tablespoons honey
2 to 3 tablespoons horseradish
1 teaspoon dry mustard
¼ teaspoon salt
Paprika

Mix ingredients together. Chill several hours to blend flavor. Serve with ham loaf or baked ham.

Lemon Sauce

1 tablespoon butter
1 well beaten egg
¾ cup honey
2 tablespoons lemon juice
⅛ teaspoon salt
grated rind of 1 lemon

Melt butter, add beaten egg, honey, lemon juice and salt. Cook in double boiler until thick, stirring contantly. Add grated lemon rind. If using this recipe for cake filling, add two eggs.

Tupelo Honey Raisin Sauce

1 cup raisins
½ cup water
1 cup tupelo honey
1 teaspoon lemon juice

Cook raisins in water very slowly until raisins are soft, but not mushy. Add honey and lemon juice and serve over hot meal as a delicious nutrition-boosting sauce.

VEGETABLES

Acorn Squash

Bake halves of acorn squash, cut side down on a
greased baking dish for 30 minutes in 375° oven.
Turn over, coat top edges and the cavity with butter
and honey. Sprinkle with nutmeg. Continue baking
for about 15 more minutes

Carrots

    6 large carrots
    ¼ cup butter
    ¼ cup prepared mustard
    ½ cup honey
    2 tablespoons chopped chives or parsley
      salt & pepper

Cook carrots which have been cut in slices. Drain.
Blend and cook other ingredients. Cover carrots
and heat to serving temperature.

Corn

    3 tablespoons butter
    1 medium onion—chopped
    1 medium green pepper—diced
    4 cups fresh corn kernels from cobs
    ¼ cup water
    1 tablespoon honey
    1 teaspoon salt
    2 tablespoons chopped pimento
    ½ cup grated cheese or crisp
      crumbled cooked bacon

Melt butter in frying pan. Saute onions and green
pepper until tender. Add corn, water, honey,
seasoning and pimento. Cover and simmer until
corn is cooked. Stir several times. Serve hot with
cheese or bacon.

Honeyed Beets

Make a sauce of:

> 2 tablespoons butter
> 2 tablespoons flour
> 2 tablespoons honey
> ½ cup vinegar
> ½ cup water

Cook until thick. Pour over beets, sliced or diced.

Honeyed Sweet Potatoes

Boil 6 medium sized sweet potatoes with jackets left on. Drain when tender and remove skins. Cut in half lengthwise. Arrange in a buttered baking dish. Heat together:

> ½ cup honey
> ¼ cup butter
> ½ cup orange juice

Add this sauce to potatoes and bake in a quick oven about 400° until brown.

Mixed Bean Casserole

> 1 large can baked beans (without tomato sauce)
> 1 large can red kidney beans (drained)
> 1 large can green lima beans (drained)
> ¼ cup chopped onion
> ¼ cup shortening
> ¼ cup wine vinegar
> ¼ cup water
> ¼ cup honey
> 1 teaspoon dry mustard
> 1 teaspoon salt
> ½ cup chili sauce or ketchup

Mix all ingredients in a large casserole dish and bake at 300° for two hours, stirring after first half hour to mix well. This may be cooked in electric frying pan if desired.

Onions

Peel four large onions, cut in half and parboil for about 10 minutes. Drain. Mix together:

 ¼ cup honey
 ¼ cup vinegar
 2 tablespoons salad oil
 1 teaspoon dry mustard
 ½ teaspoon salt
 ½ teaspoon paprika

Pour this over onions in a frying pan and simmer about ½ hour. Serve sauce over the onions.

Orange and Lemon Beets

 3 lbs fresh beets or 2 cans of beets
 ¼ cup lemon juice
 ½ cup orange juice
 2 tablespoons wine vinegar
 2 tablespoons honey
 1½ tablespoons cornstarch
   salt & pepper
 ¼ cup butter
 ½ teaspoon grated orange peel (optional)
 ½ teaspoon grated lemon peel (optional)

Drain sliced beets very well. Combine fruit juices, vinegar, honey, cornstarch and seasonings in a saucepan. Stir until smooth and bring to a boil, cooking until thick and clear. Add beets, butter and peel. Heat to serving temperature.

Small Onions

Cook about 24 small onions in water for 20 minutes. Drain and put in casserole covered with the following sauce:

- 2 tablespoons honey
- 2 tablespoons ketchup
- 3 tablespoons butter
- ¼ cup hot water
  - salt & pepper or cayenne

Bake in 350° oven for about one hour. Casserole to be covered.

Turnips

Mix equal quantities of honey and butter in a saucepan. Heat and add a diced unpeeled apple. Cook for about 5 minutes, then add cooked turnip chunks and glaze.

MISCELLANEOUS

Buttermilk Pancakes

    1 eggs
    1¼ cups buttermilk or sour milk
    2 tablespoons soft shortening
    1¼ cups flour
    1 tablespoon honey
    1 teaspoon baking powder
    ½ teaspoon soda
    ½ teaspoon salt

Beat egg well and add remaining ingredients—
beating until smooth. Bake on hot griddle.

Cinnamon Toast

    1 tablespoon honey
    1 tablespoon butter
    ½ teaspoon cinnamon

Blend together. This is enough for one slice of toast.

Cranberry Relish

    1 quart raw cranberries
    2 oranges
    4 apples
    2 cups honey

Put all the fruit through the food chopper. Add the
honey and mix well. Store in a covered jar in a cool
place. Delicious when served with turkey, chicken
or pork.

Doughnuts

Heat kettle of fat 365°

1 cup honey
2 tablespoons shortening
1 egg, well beaten
2 tablespoons baking powder
1 cup sweet milk
1 teaspoon salt
½ teaspoon ginger
flour

Cream shortening and honey. Add egg. Sift baking powder, salt and ginger with one cup of flour. Add milk alternately with flour to make a dough which may be rolled out and cut. Roll the dough to ½ inch thick, and cut with doughnut cutter. Cook in hot fat until nicely browned. Drain on paper towelling.

Ham Waffles

2 cups milk
2 eggs
2 tablespoons honey
⅓ cup melted shortening
2 cups pancake mix
1 cup diced cooked ham

Mix batter until smooth. Stir in ham. Bake in hot waffle iron until steaming stops. Serve with Honey Butter.

Honey Butter

Delicious on hot biscuits, bread, waffles, pancakes.

Blend 1 cup of honey with ½ cup butter.

This may stored in covered container in refrigerator.

Oat Muffins

Preheat oven to 400°

2 tablespoons butter
1 egg
¾ cup sour milk
1 teaspoon salt
2 teaspoons baking powder
4 tablespoons honey
1 cup oatmeal
1½ cups flour
½ teaspoon soda

Cream butter and honey, add beaten egg, then the oatmeal. Mix dry ingredients and sift into mixture alternately with sour milk. Bake in greased muffin tins for 30 minutes in a hot oven. ¼ cup chopped dates or raisins may be added if desired.

CONCLUSION

"Let Us Hear The Conclusion of The Matter", said King Solomon, and so say I. While modern science has not yet proved (nor, indeed, fully disproved) all the virtues that have been claimed for honey since recorded history, nonetheless some general statements can be made with full assurance.

Honey is sweet. No one would attempt to deny it. But more, honey is food—incredibly rich food nutritionally, and bio-chemically ideal as a food for man. And no one would attempt to deny that either.

By contrast, refined sugar has no nutritional value. Calories, yes, and sweetening power yes, but vitamins, minerals, and enzymes—no. True, it's inexpensive. But then so is honey, relatively, and just as abundant—and just as versatile.

Honey does have therapeutic value. To what extent, and for what specific purpose may vary from individual to individual, and from circumstance to circumstance. Modern medicine uses it, but sparingly. But "the people" use it abundantly, just as it has been used for untold generations and for almost every conceivable reason, and there seems to be no valid reason why it should not be used.

Indeed, in all the generations that honey has been used as a healer I doubt the number of cases of adverse reaction *all put together* would equal the number of disastrous results that come to light *daily* in the testing of modern drugs.

So even if a dose of honey doesn't cure your sneeze, at least you need have little fear it will kill or maim you either.

I thank God for this wonderful country in which each man has freedom of choice of religion, politics, and his preference for food and drink and medicine, and I pray this may never change. America, I love you.

And Honey, I love you, too; you're so sweet and good to me.

Add Your Own Recipes

_____

_____

_____

_____

_____

_____

_____

_____

_____

_____

_____

_____

_____

_____

_____

_____

_____

_____

_____

_____

_____

_____